HE
SINGS
FOR US

A Sociolinguistic Analysis of the Appalachian Subculture and of Jesse Stuart as a Major American Author

John Howard Spurlock

Editorial Assistance
Dr. Joseph A. Glaser

UNIVERSITY
PRESS OF
AMERICA

D1258333

Library of Congress Cataloging in Publication Data

Spurlock, John Howard.
    He sings for us.

    1. Stuart, Jesse, 1907-   --Criticism and
interpretation. 2. Appalachian region, Southern,
in literature. 3. Appalachian region, Southern--
Social life and customs. I. Title.
PS3537.T92516Z87   818'.5209   80-22076
ISBN 0-8191-1271-2
ISBN 0-8191-1272-0 (pbk.)

Acknowledgment is made to the following sources
for permission to reprint from material already
published:

Hold April by Jesse Stuart. Copyright (c) 1962
by Jesse Stuart. Used with the permission of
McGraw-Hill Book Company.

Daughter of the Legend by Jesse Stuart. Copyright (c) 1965 by Jesse Stuart. Used with the permission of McGraw-Hill Book Company.

"It is most painful now as I" by Jesse Stuart.
Reprinted from THE SATURDAY EVENING POST (c) 1959
The Curtis Publishing Company.

"The Crow's Dark Night" by Jesse Stuart. Reprinted from SOUTHWEST Review, April 1967.

For all other quotations from the writings of
Jesse Stuart, permission granted by Jesse Stuart.

To Naomi Deane Stuart

Appalachia's First Lady

BOOKS BY JESSE STUART

Autobiographical

Beyond Dark Hills	1938
The Thread That Runs So True	1949
The Year of My Rebirth	1956
God's Oddling	1960
Mr. Gallion's School	1967
To Teach, To Love	1970
The Kingdom Within	1979

Poetry

Harvest of Youth	1930
Man With a Bull-Tongue Plow	1934
Album of Destiny	1944
Kentucky Is My Land	1952
Hold April	1962
Autumn Lovesong	1971
The World of Jesse Stuart (edited by J. R. LeMaster)	1975
The Seasons of Jesse Stuart	1976

Novels

Trees of Heaven	1940
Taps For Private Tussie	1943
Foretaste of Glory	1946
Mongrel Mettle	1944
Hie to the Hunters	1950
The Good Spirit of Laurel Ridge	1953
Daughter of the Legend	1965
The Land Beyond the River	1973

Short Stories

Head O'W-Hollow	1936
Men of the Mountains	1941
Tales from the Plum Grove Hills	1946
Clearing in the Sky & Other Stories	1950
Plowshare in Heaven	1958

A Jesse Stuart Harvest	1965
My Land Has a Voice	1966
Come Gentle Spring	1969
Dawn of Remembered Spring	1972
32 Votes Before Breakfast	1974
The Short Stories	
(edited and annotated by Kenzo	
Soneda and Norio Shimamura)	1974

Collections

A Jesse Stuart Reader	1963
(stories and poems)	
Save Every Lamb	1964
(animal tales)	
Come Back to the Farm	1971
(stories and articles)	
My World	1975
(essays)	
Lost Sandstones and Lonely Skies	1979
(essays)	
If I Were Seventeen Again	1980
(essays)	

Children's Books

Tim	1939
The Beatinest Boy	1953
A Penny's Worth of Character	1954
Red Mule	1955
The Rightful Owner	1960
Huey, the Engineer	1960
Andy Finds a Way	1961
A Ride with Huey, the Engineer	1966
Old Ben	1970
Come to My Tomorrowland	1971

For a more complete and descriptive listing of Stuart's works, see Jesse and Jane Stuart; A Bibliography, compiled by Hensley C. Woodbridge. Murray State University Printing Services, 1979, 221 pages.

ACKNOWLEDGMENTS

Analyzing a culture and the literary spokesman of a culture is a difficult task; analyzing an author who has published as prolifically as Jesse Stuart adds to the difficulty. The first draft of He Sings For Us was well over 300 pages--mainly because of the many excellent examples of Stuart's work. Dr. Joseph A. Glaser, my friend and colleague at Western Kentucky University, worked tirelessly with me in reducing this book to 200 pages. To him I owe a great deal of gratitude.

Numerous colleagues at W.K.U. have assisted me in this work by granting me two fellowships and two reduced-class semesters, by furnishing me with suggestions and materials, and by encouraging me in the progress of the work. I would like to thank particulary the following individuals: Dr. James Heldman, Dr. Robert Mounce, Dr. James Davis, Dr. John Minton, Dr. Curtis Logsdon, Dr. George McCelvey, Dr. Lowell Harrison, Dr. Jim Wayne Miller, Miss Addie Hochstrasser, and Mrs. Dianne Rutledge.

I owe special thanks to Dr. K. M. Heim of the Murray State University Library, the present greatest depository of Stuart material. During my research at Murray, Dr. Heim provided me with an office, typewriter, library assistants, and suggestions.

To Dr. David Maurer, Professor Emeritus, University of Louisville, one of America's greatest criminal linguists, I owe inexpressable gratitude. Professor Maurer introduced me to methods of analysis in linguistics and socio-linguistics. For his expert tutelage, I join countless of his former students in saying, "Thanks, Doc!"

To Dr. Harold Richardson of the University of Louisville and Chairman of The Jesse Stuart Foundation, I express my thanks for having been given the opportunity to present an overview of

He *Sings For Us* at "The Greenbo Sessions," the greatest critical symposium on Stuart ever held.

I am indebted to Dr. Hensley C. Woodbridge for his bibliography of Jesse and Jane Stuart—a source invaluable to serious Stuart scholars.

I express my gratitude to Jesse and Naomi Stuart for answering my many correspondences and for the use of much of the copyrighted material in this book.

I sincerely thank the following presses and publications for their cooperation in regard to copyrighted material: The University Press of Kentucky; Little, Brown and Company; McGraw-Hill Book Company, Inc.; Hallmark Cards, Inc.; E. P. Dutton and Company, Inc.; The Curtis Publishing Company; and SOUTHWEST *Review*.

All photographs are from the private collection of Jesse and Naomi Stuart. I extend my deep gratitude to the Stuarts, The Jesse Stuart Foundation, and The Kentucky Department of Public Information for their cooperation in the use of these photographs, and to Robert Stuart of Russellville, Kentucky, for his excellent reproduction of the photographs.

Every book is a collaboration; of collaborators, I have had the best. I thank them all.

John Howard Spurlock

HE SINGS FOR US: A SOCIOLINGUISTIC ANALYSIS OF THE APPALACHIAN SUBCULTURE AND OF JESSE STUART AS A MAJOR AMERICAN AUTHOR

INTRODUCTION

In the course of one of the longest and most distinguished careers in American literature, Jesse Stuart has had over 3,000 publications, including more than 50 books--32 of which are still in print, 460 short stories, 2100 poems, and 400 articles. His work has appeared in our most prestigious literary magazines and in over 225 anthologies of American literature; his novels have been called classics and one has been selected as a Masterpiece of World Literature; he is a Fellow of the Academy of American Poets; he has been nominated for a Pulitzer Prize; one of his books of poems has been named one of the 100 best books in America and one of the 1000 great books of the world; and he has received many of America's highest scholastic and literary awards. Stuart holds fifteen honorary doctoral degrees, and his works have achieved a world-wide readership, several of them having been translated and printed on six continents. And yet, in spite of his phenomenal record of accomplishments, the literary merit of his work is still debated. Stuart has said the question appears to be, "Am I a popular writer or am I a literary writer?"[1]

This book is an attempt to document Stuart's excellence as a literary artist, and at the same time investigate the lack of recognition his work has received, through a close consideration of facets of the Appalachian subculture embedded in his writing. It is my thesis that Stuart is a great literary artist because of the profound accuracy with which his work mirrors the Appalachian world and that the critical neglect that has hampered his reputation is due largely to cultural bias--the failure of critics from the dominant culture to understand or grant literary interest to the particular subculture from which he writes.

Early in my research on the Appalachian subculture and the literature of Jesse Stuart, it became apparent to me that both scholars of Appalachian linguistics and the majority of Stuart critics

1

had overlooked the fact that culture and behavior are interwoven. Throughout the research I have tried always to hold in mind Edward T. Hall's statement of this vital fact in The Silent Language: "Culture controls behavior in deep and persisting ways, many of which are outside of awareness and therefore beyond conscious control of the individual. When the anthropologist stresses this point he is usually ignored, for he is challenging the deepest popular beliefs about ourselves as well as foreigners. He leads people to see things they might not want to see."[2]

During the composition of He Sings For Us, I have been asked by colleagues, giving professional advice, if the book were a study of the Appalachian subculture or of Jesse Stuart. The book, of absolute necessity, is both: there has been little understanding of Appalachia as a subculture, even among linguists--less among Stuart critics--and the picturesque-speech, the folksy craftsy, and the urbanite's weekend-guide approaches to Jesse Stuart and the quaint Appalachian culture have done him great disservice. The vast majority of those writing Stuart criticism have no knowledge of Appalachia as a linguistic subculture with a well-established and continuing historic tradition that defines the Appalachian ethos. Other Stuart critics have encountered major basic themes in Stuart's work, explicable by a knowledge of the Appalachian subculture, and asked the question--"Why?"

In trying to answer this question, to describe the rich and detailed relationship between Stuart's work and the Appalachian culture that underlies it, I have been guided by ten indices, or salient characteristics, proposed by George L. Trager for the analysis of particular cultures and determination of their special features. Trager suggests that the shape of a culture can be traced by investigating its approach to interaction, territoriality, association, subsistence, exploitation of resources, bisexuality, education, recreation, temporality, and defense.

Wherever he is, man acts upon his environment and it acts upon him. This leads to interaction

2

with the environment or territory and with other
life within the environment--association. A certain amount of work is undertaken in any culture
in order to provide subsistence, and the forms of
work arise from the exploitation of resources at
hand. The male and female roles (bisexuality) are
central issues in every culture, and some learning
(education) mechanism is always present: this process, whether it be formal or informal, is the
basis for enculturation--becoming a member of the
group. A certain amount of play or recreation is
always present and is a basic cultural activity.
A culture's temporal concept arises from its arrangement of work and play within its particular
environment. And in every culture there appears
to be an inborn defense mechanism of protecting
oneself and the cultural system from other cultural
systems.3 By analyzing each of these areas of
value and behavior in the Appalachian subculture
and Stuart's reflections of these in his works, I
hope to suggest how deeply rooted his art is in
the region, achieving universal merit through its
absolute truth to the particular.

Jesse Stuart, being highly educated and having
traveled throughout the world, has been aware of
the fact that the Appalachian subculture is different than the dominant culture of industrialized
and urbanized twentieth-century America. Moreover,
in portraying the human tragedy and comedy of his
highland literary world and the strangely familiar
characters who dwell there, Stuart has accurately
and imaginatively recorded the irreversible impact
the dominant culture has had upon both the real and
his fictional Appalachia. He has captured the whole
linguistic subculture in all of its ramifications
in three literary genres: poetry, short story, and
the novel (autobiographical and fictional). It is
the complexity this rich cultural background has
given his art that makes him a great author, and
one who is capable of speaking to all men.

As is true of William Faulkner's, Jesse
Stuart's chosen literary region is particular but
it is inhabited by the family of man. Jesse Stuart's
world of W-Hollow is his Dublin and Jefferson, and

he writes from his hill-rimmed locale to the world. He Sings For Us is a study of the Appalachian sub-culture and of a major American author--Jesse Hilton Stuart.

NOTES

1. Shirley Williams, "Jesse Stuart: a Kentucky writer with a zest for life and letters at 70 despite setbacks," The Courier-Journal & Times Magazine (Louisville, Ky.), 7 August 1977, p. 11.

2. Edward T. Hall, The Silent Language (New York: Fawcett World Library, 1963), p. 35.

3. George L. Trager, "Language in Culture," Encyclopedia Britannica, 1955 ed., pp. 696-699.

Jesse Stuart with neighbor, Leonard Darby (left), and father "Little Mitch" Stuart, and Jerry B.

CHAPTER ONE

ASSOCIATION, INTERACTION, AND DEFENSE

Association, interaction, and defense are closely interwoven in Jesse Stuart's depiction of Appalachia. It is the rules governing community life in the region and participation in its complex system of reference groups that make the Appalachian socially distinctive. This distinctiveness, in turn, accounts for the misunderstanding and anguish that have marked Appalachians' interaction with the dominant culture. And the fierce loyalties and frustrations produced by these two forces are behind the Appalachian subculture's extraordinary emphasis on defense--defense of the nation in time of war, and equally vigorous defense of the subculture's right to exist within the nation. Stuart's work does full justice to each of these characteristics.

Association, the code of behavior that defines relationships within a culture, is more responsible than any of the other indices for an individual's sense of belonging, of being a member of a race apart. Appalachians are particularly blessed with this sense, and throughout his career Jesse Stuart has written widely on the separate heritage and identity of his people, an "original culture within a country's culture." "The highlanders," he has said, "are so different economically, culturally, and politically from other residents of the seven states where they live--West Virginia, Virginia, North Carolina, Kentucky, Tennessee, Georgia, Alabama--that we have often threatened to secede and form an independent Highland State."[1]

Appalachians expand the usual notion of association, moreover, to include the past. As Stuart knows, much of what Appalachia is today is intelligible only in terms of the Appalachians who have gone before: "The pioneers of eastern Kentucky mountains were mainly of Scotch, English, and Irish descent. They were hard fighting, hard drinking,

7

God-fearing poor people, handy with ax, mattock, spade and hoe, accurate with the old flintlock hunting rifle, steady behind the handles of the bull-tongue plows. . . . It is an evident fact that it will be many years before the mountaineers of eastern Kentucky develop into a polite tea-drinking, . . . group of people. The heritage they have behind them is not what a great-great-grandfather . . . did. If they start tracing back in family history they usually find more than they want to make public."[2]

The genealogy of Stuart's Appalachians furnishes vital insight into the land and its people: "These early settlers, those who received land and those who didn't, settled this land primarily to build homes. They were 'anti-crown,' 'anti-king,' and 'anti-queen'--a fiercely patriotic group of settlers whose former ancestry, English, Scottish, Welsh and Irish stemmed from the British Isles." These Appalachians developed a deep love of place-- of mountains, ridges, streams, valleys, and family cemeteries of the high hills--and they left an indelible stamp on the culture they passed along to their mountain descendants.[3]

The solidarity of Appalachians stems not only from their reverence for the past but from their membership in a richly stratified contemporary culture. In Appalachia everyone knows there are rules governing behavior. The structure of Appalachian society is composed of reference groups consisting of the family, friends, and friendly neighbors. While families are strongly patriarchal, in reference groups involving peers the proceedings are democratic. All members participate and everyone has his say. Leaders are recognized but everyone tries to improve his position by engaging in the art of conversation. These groups, especially those that encourage active participation, provide a strong sense of belonging, and they are remarkably stable. Potentially explosive subjects are avoided because the relationship is personal and each participant has an innate understanding of how far he can go. Furthermore, the stability of the group is backed up by appropriate sanctions. Should any member overstep the mark, there is an explosion

8

which, to an outsider, seems disproportionate.
Expulsion from the group means loss of social life,
security and individuality.

The central importance of reference groups in
Appalachian life is shown by the seriousness with
which they are treated. Unlike milder forms of
ostracism in the dominant culture, rifts that arise
in Appalachian reference groups take a long time
to heal, if they ever do at all. Jack Weller has
strongly emphasized this aspect of Appalachian
association in Yesterday's People: "Let everyone
who works in the Appalachian South take cognizance
of the power of these reference groups, which stand
at the very center of the mountaineer's life. To
step out of the group would mean loss of identity.
To stand out in the group or to try to change the
group from within is practically impossible, for
one would quickly be ostracized. Any outsider who
tries to change the reference group is very likely
to find himself rejected by it."[4]

In addition to his awareness of the importance
of association with the past, Jesse Stuart gives a
clear picture of the role of contemporary reference
groups in Appalachian life. Many of his characters,
in particular, find themselves holding the unenvia-
ble position of divided loyalty to conflicting reference groups where complete loyalty to one demands
expulsion from the other. The narrator of Beyond
Dark Hills is caught between the worlds of his
grandfather (a Democrat and rebel) and his father
(a Republican and yankee). Tarvin Bushman in Trees
of Heaven stands between his landgrabbing father
and the tenant family of his beloved Subrinea Tussie.
Father Mick Stuart and son James Stuart in God's
Oddling tell the formally educated Jesse that he
is an "oddlin" (odd one) because he does not share
their beloved tastebud tobacco or drink with them
from the moonshine jug. When Dave Stoneking in
Daughter of the Legend marries Deutsia Huntoon and
is loyal to her family, he becomes an outcast to
his best friend and to the people of Oak Hill.

Grandpa Tussie, the venerated leader of the
'Welfare Tussies,' discovers that the reference
group loyalty can sometimes be shifting and

9

uncertain. He spends practically all of his dead
son's war-insurance money in entertaining, lodging,
and feeding hordes of Tussies in his rented "man-
sion" only to be reported by them and thus lose his
beloved welfare benefits and his political clout.[5]

The humor of many Stuart stories, as is true
of much of the humor in the Appalachian subculture,
results from the characters seeing how far they can
stretch reference group loyalty without overstep-
ping proscribed limits. In "Road Number One" Pa
"works his tail off" to help elect Toodle Powell
as county judge only to discover that Judge Powell
will not fix Pa's road. The judge knows he has Pa
trapped, a man who talked so earnestly in the judge's
behalf. Most reference group rules are stretched
to the breaking point during trading and horse
swapping. In "Horse-trading Trembles" Pa is beaten
badly by Eif Sizemore, the greatest horse trader
in that country, who trades Pa a "heavie" (short-
winded) horse for two mule colts and $20 boot. Eif
is in turn "skinned" by a young boy who tells him
the unadorned truth--something Eif cannot deal with.[6]
In "Remember the Sabbath Day and Keep it Holy,"
young Sherd Jason exceeds the reference group's
range of tolerated behavior in wrapping a blacksnake
around Old Red Brady's neck. Brady puts around 100
no. 8 shot in the fleeing Jason's rump.[7]

But the primary reference group in Appalachia,
the greatest source of the sense of belonging, and
the most powerful force in the continuation of the
subculture is the family. "How to Thread a Needle"
is a vital Stuart short story that explores the
truly remarkable cohesive power exerted by the Appalachian family, a power that can overcome individual
differences or social and historical change. The
boy narrator Jasper Baines offers us a viewpoint
within such a family. He is fully aware of the
differences that threaten to divide the group, but
he also feels the blood loyalty that successfully
resists them.

The plot of the story involves Grandpa Baines,
the bearded patriarch of the clan, and his calling
together of armed Baines men to travel to the Homeland Graveyard at Big Beechie in Darter County to

lie in nightly ambush for the supposed rival clan who are desecrating the graves of the Baines dead by pushing over their tombstones. When no enemy appears during the nights of the deadly Baines wake, the men go home, deciding the wind to be the culprit of desecration. In this story of little external action, the reader gains precious insight through the eyes of Jasper Baines into the three generations of Appalachians and their different attitudes toward 'proper' association within the subculture. The three generations differ in views and values but the cohesive force of family is able to override such differences and hold the family unit together.

Grandpa Baines is the embodiment of the old Appalachian of an eye for an eye. His black-eyes are "as mean as bull's eyes" and he is so angry at the supposed desecration that he walks around "like a rooster." He does not ask his sons and grandsons if they will join him in the feud; he tells them to get their guns, and it is understood that "Pap" will get the first shot at the opposing clan. Grandpa fondles his rifle "like a mother fondles her child." As is true of many older Appalachians, Grandpa views most modern technological improvement as bad, and he hates modern machinery.

> "But your car is not ahead of the old mule, hoss and cattle teams," Grandpa said. "We aint ahead of the people then because the mules, hosses, and cattle breathed air and they liked people and we liked them. They were alive. This car aint alive. It's a dead thing that can't talk and eat and it can't breathe air."[8]

Jasper's father Cy is representative of second-generation Appalachians--hardworking farmers who adapt to advancing technology. He is a fine marksman but unlike his father he does not concern himself with the supposed slight to his family; as a working farmer he does not view machinery as a bad thing. Lacking Grandpa's extreme violence, Cy, however, will not tolerate personal insult:

"Watch about driving so fast! You
might burn it up!"
"If I had hold of that joy bird I'd
burn him up," Pa said. "It makes me
awful mad to have somebody a-hollerin
at me on the highway. I don't like
these smart boys." (23)

Jasper is the third-generation Appalachian.
He can hit a dime at twenty-five paces with his
.22 rifle and he is proud of his family's mettle:
"We were tough-butted white oaks growing on rocky
slopes. There were no softwood trees among us."
He and his cousins have "the shrewd cold eyes of
the young hawks," but Jasper cannot understand his
grandfather's idea of justice for desecraters of
the family graveyard, which is to "cut'im in two
with bullets." Jasper, unlike his grandfather,
does not want to shoot family enemies for upsetting
tombstones, and he is relieved when the "wake" is
called off (16-30).

This, then, is association in the Appalachian
subculture, a subject Stuart treats honestly and
profoundly as he does every other aspect of his
region. The Appalachian's ties with his past and
with a whole range of reference groups culminating
in his sense of family create an extraordinarily
powerful social bond between him and his region.
This network of personal and family loyalties
shapes his behavior and defines his place in the
world. It is little wonder to find Appalachians
at sea when it comes to interacting with members
of the dominant culture whose social sense is dif-
ferently structured and who are, moreover, convinced
that their ways must prevail.

Jack Weller's Yesterday's People, one of the
finest analyses of the Appalachian subculture written to date, puts the problem of interaction between
Appalachia and her neighbors in a nutshell: "There
is something about a dominant culture which will
not allow a differing culture to exist side by side
with it. So long as the Southern mountaineer lived
apart in his labyrinth, he was left alone. As he
begins to emerge from the mountains, or as middle
class America begins to invade his homeland, these

well-meaning citizens feel that the mountaineer, on seeing their 'superior' culture, will immediately want to share it. For many a mountaineer, nothing could be farther from the truth . . . " (134-135).

The author, a United Presbyterian minister who lived and worked in Appalachia for thirteen years, came to these conclusions only after coming to know the unique culture of the region from the inside, the way Jesse Stuart has always known it. Weller saw, for example, that the dominant culture's tendency toward materialism and the impersonality it fosters would mean the death of the Appalachian way of life (83). But Weller is exceptional. The dominant culture has traditionally made little attempt to appreciate what Appalachia has to offer; instead, it has tried to root out what is different from itself and impose its values and attitudes on Appalachia's poor "hillbillies." As a result of this campaign for culture uniformity, neither Stuart nor his characters have fared well at the hands of the world beyond their mountains.

With the appearance of Man With A Bull-Tongue Plow in August of 1934, America had a great new literary artist, but many failed to appreciate such a different genius. The persona of sonnet 36 sings his "dead grass lines" of the "futile song" of the common people and wonders if his audience will accept his art:

> . . . If you would only listen
> Where moonlight on the green leaves glistens--
> Listen to the words like wind among the trees,
> Like winds beneath the stars and in the green leaves,
> I wonder if you'd say: "Stop singing please!"[9]

Several personas throughout Man With A Bull-Tongue Plow do not succeed in the dominant culture's process of acculturation, and they return home to literally save their souls. The persona of sonnet 209 has haunting memories of wandering through a southern town penniless, lonely and hungry. The persona of sonnet 212 has "grown hungry" for the hills, skies, and trees of home, and he wants to put his arms around the black oak trees. Sonnet 233 pictures the persona returning home to Appalachia for a rebirth:

> There I shall dive into a deeper stream
> And I shall drown or come up with a dream.

Many narrators in Stuart's novels experience cultural rejection. For the majority of Appalachians the dominant culture is not represented by Chicago, Detroit, New York, and so forth. It consists of urbanized Appalachians living in Appalachian villages and cities and conforming to the essential dominant-culture pattern of behavior. In direct contrast are the Appalachians of the traditional subculture--those rural people who live on the ridges and on the steep hillside farms. As narrator of Beyond Dark Hills, Jesse Stuart describes his initial reaction to the city high school students of Greenup High. Stuart, from remote Womack Hollow, ate his lunch of cornbread and ham in private because he didn't want others to see this humble fare and, noticing their finer clothes, he cut crossties so that he could afford to dress as nicely.[10] Peg Sparks, in Hie to the Hunters, has his family referred to as a "den of hillbillies" by Mr. Hargis, an irate Greenwood merchant who demands that Peg return his son, a city lad who is quite free to go home any time he pleases.[11]

Of all of Stuart's characters, perhaps Dave Stoneking of Daughter of the Legend suffers most from the vicious and mindless cycle of acculturation. Dave attempts to stand between the contiguous worlds of Appalachia and the dominant culture, and he is badly hurt. Dave is from a middle-class Virginia family and he cuts timber with his boyhood friend Ben Dewberry in Cantwell County, near Oak Hill, Tennessee. He falls in love with and marries Deutsia Huntoon, a beautiful olive-skinned, golden-haired girl from Sanctuary Mountain whose people are referred to as "Melungeons"--a mysterious race of people. Dave loses Ben's friendship, the friend-

14

ship of the townspeople, and Deutsia's life because of the cross-cultural marriage.

These and many additional Stuart personas, narrators and characters would have little difficulty understanding the sentiments expressed by Mart Tussie in _Album of Destiny_. Mart regrets having done so much killing and having whored his life away in the type of living that hardens the heart. Mart left home to live life hard in the dominant culture, and he is the embodiment of the sheer cultural shock so many Appalachians experience in a dominant culture of winding and unwinding bobbins. Mart is truly a mountain hawk loose in a world where he can no longer hear his highland falconer:

> My heart got harder than our cellar
> wall
> Until I've seen horned Devils in
> dark places.[12]

Much of the humor in Stuart's short stories arises from his artistic juxtaposition of the dominant culture and the Appalachian subculture. "Competition at Slush Creek" is typical of Stuart's rare ability to narrate from a borderline between these two worlds and laugh in both directions.

In "Competition at Slush Creek" Franklin Foster and Marvin Clayton, thematic representations of the dominant culture, are rival Blakesburg undertakers who often race to the homes of mountain corpses. Marvin has an instinct for death but Franklin has the speed. In the race for the body at Slush Creek, Franklin leads--traveling 90 on the straightaway, 70 on the wrong side of curves, and sounding his siren continuously. He arrives too early--between the men of sheriff Bert Saddler's posse and the Sandless clan as they square off on opposite sides of the hollow road in a shoot out.[13]

Throughout his career of portraying the Appalachian subculture, Stuart has occasionally been accused of exaggeration. This false charge arises from the gap between the dominant culture and daily reality in Appalachia. Typical is "The Moon Child from Wolfe Creek"--the story of a boy who was afraid

of the schoolhouse. This story was originally a
chapter in The Thread That Runs So True, but Stuart
omitted it before sending the manuscript to the
publishers: he did not feel that people would accept the moon child as a believable character.
After Thread was published Stuart talked to several
teachers who had taught students "wild as a fox"--
students who never adjusted to the regimen of school
and classwork.

Don Crump, the "moon child" from Wolfe Creek,
will come as near as the clearing above Lonesome
Valley School and pace nervously back and forth;
his behavior resembles that of a trapped animal in
a cage. The pupils believe Don is a moon child--
"born when the moon is tilted in the sky." The
teacher realizes that Don must come to the school,
that greatest acculturator of all men, totally as
an act of his own free will:

> But on Monday afternoon, of my first month
> at Lonesome Valley, Don Crump came inside
> the schoolhouse. He walked inside, looked
> quickly at all the pupils, at the windows,
> then at the door. He held a cap in his
> hand when he sat down on a back seat. He
> acted as if he were ready to run. My pupils
> were naturally excited when he came inside,
> and started looking at him. I motioned
> for them to look toward my desk and to keep
> quiet and pay no attention to Don Crump.
> His was the eternal hunger and thirst of
> youth for laughter, play, recreation, as-
> sociation and enjoyment upon this earth.
> Don had come to us. We hadn't run him
> down, tied his hands and feet and brought
> him to us either. He had come of his own
> accord.[14]

Cultural patterns go deep--to the center of the
human psyche. Stuart's Appalachians visit the dominant culture or stay in it to make a living, but
as is true of one persona of Kentucky is My Land
the hills had the child and the city cannot have
the man. The Appalachian sees the smokestacks of
eastern industry, the "cliff dwellings" of New
York--its deep gorges of streets and avenues--and

16

longs for the land of log shacks and lonesome waters.[15]

Another facet of interaction is Appalachia's exploitation at the hands of the dominant culture. The rape of Appalachia began in the latter half of the nineteenth century and continues today, and because of it the Appalachian mistrusts representatives of the dominant culture: employers, the government, legal officials, and social workers. Having lost his timber and coal, and often his right to control what is done to his own land and home, the Appalachian views all "official" representatives as "them" rather than "us". As has been dramatically stated by Don West in Appalachia in the Sixties, Appalachians are aware that they have been economically exploited by the dominant culture: ". . . the southern mountains have been missionarized, researched, studied, romanticized, dramatized, hillbillyized, Dog-patched and poverty-ized again. . . . Southern Appalachia is a colonial possession of Eastern based industry. Like all exploited colonial areas, the 'mother country' may make generous gestures now and then, send missionaries with up-lift programs, 'superior' religion, build churches and sometimes schools. They'll do about everything--except get off the backs of the people, end the exploitive domination. That, the people themselves must eventually see to."[16]

About the only way the mountain people have of resisting such "progress" is to cling to their personal independence of spirit. Throughout his literature, Stuart reflects the Appalachian's refusal to march to the quick click of raw efficiency in the economic system of the dominant culture. Traditionally, Appalachians who have worked for "The Man" in the coal mines and in large industrial cities have gained the reputation of being hard-working people. But they have refused to be subservient to bosses, and they walk away from good jobs when to remain is to suffer the loss of their precious individual liberty and the right to tell any tyrannical boss to "go to hell." Success at any price is an unknown concept to Stuart's freedom-loving Appalachians. Rance Bushman is glad to have quit his job and to have returned to the restoring

17

mountains of home from the rush, roar, grabbing
hooks, and big bosses of the steel mill:

I have come home a mountain-flowing river
To flow and flow among these pine-clad hills.[17]

Mumford Sowards Jr. says that coal officials who
frown upon miners' unions would gladly join the
C.I.O. or X.Y.Z. if they had to crawl on their
bellies through sulphured slime and rats for
"death-colored wages" for their family's bread.[18]

Merciless economic exploitation of Appalachia
and Appalachians in their interaction with the
dominant culture is a recurrent theme running
throughout Stuart's literature, but perhaps the
short story "The Anglo Saxons of Auxierville" presents his hardest-hitting picture of what this exploitation has done to the lives of Stuart's people.

Narrator Shan Powderjay leaves his mountain
farm home to visit his cousin Mick Powderjay, a
coal miner whose father sold all the family land
to the coal company:

"Pa sold all the land the Govermint gave
his great-grandpa fer fightin in the Revolution. He sold the mineral rights fer a
quarter an acre. Then he sold the land."[19]

The coal camp of Auxierville is the Appalachian
Inferno, where all who enter abandon hope. It is
a Hell of eleven railroad tracks across a narrow
valley where miners sit in the shade of their
narrow "shotgun houses" and squint their "ferrety
eyes" at God's light through a mist of coal dust.
It is a "town" where men work seven days a week and
overtime and are too busy to take their sons fishing
in the polluted Sandy River. It is a "town" where
little girls in tattered dresses walk down autumn-
dusty roads--their little sweaty legs covered in
layers of coal dust. It is the burial ground for
too many of a once proud race:

These young Anglo-Saxon girls will marry
Anglo-Saxon boys and like their mothers
will reproduce. . . . The young boys, now

in dresses and rompers, will throttle the
big engines, oil their pistons, build new
tracks, and run electric motors in the
mines. They will go back under the mountains and gravel the coal with picks, coal
cutters, and load it with shovels and
loaders. They will bring coal from the
bowels of the mountains. They will load
it in buggies and shoot the black diamonds
down to the empty cars from the tipples.
They will die natural and unnatural deaths.
They will be buried deep in Anglo-Saxon
sandrock, under Auxier County skies. . . .
The last remnants of merry old England
under the wide and spacious skies of great
America. (207-218)

In their interaction with the dominant culture,
several Stuart characters become masters at a double
standard of behavior in all money matters. Doshie
Hammertight does not steal in her Appalachian subculture because she would be committing cultural
suicide, but she thinks it is very funny to steal
food from the refrigerator of the townspeople she
works for.[20] Grandpa Tussie, leader of the "welfare Tussies," loves to watch the dispensers of
welfare commodities fight to serve him: he knows
they appreciate his political clout.[21] Uncle Peter
Skelton and the Perkins family ride the welfare
system for all it's worth because they think it is
silly.[22] The Perkins family moved from Kentucky
to Ohio where they are encouraged to exploit the
welfare system to ruination by their hardworking
taxpaying neighbors, who are sick of the whole
mess.[23]

Jesse Stuart and the Appalachian subculture
ask for two things from the dominant culture: a
good school system and factories in Appalachia.
They have received neither. Blatantly unfair assessment of hundreds of thousands of acres of coal
property robs the schools of vital revenue, and
politicians make no real effort to attract heavy
industry, which would automatically create an independent Appalachian middle class.

Stuart has fought valiantly against the dominant

culture's false economic stereotypes, which persistently portray the Appalachian as a shiftless
and lazy mountaineer, and occasionally even Stuart
has become weary of the battle:

> Sir: I read your editorial, "Schools for
> the Mountaineers" (The New Republic, April
> 4), and I'm glad somebody has the right
> opinion of the hill people. I really think
> you hit the nail on the head when you say
> they are an independent sort of people and
> rebuke charity. I think people from the
> East and North have been very unfair in
> some of their criticisms of the hill peo-
> ple. They are unfair because they do not
> know anything about us. One sentence in
> the editorial went something like this,
> "They say they are unhappy and uprooted
> in their own mountain valleys," meaning
> of course, after they'd gone to college.
> If this is true, why have colleges for the
> mountaineers? Let them alone to plow their
> own mountain valleys. Leave them alone on
> the soil--leave them there without a college
> education. . . . The happiest people I've
> ever seen have been the people living on
> little hill farms raising enough foodstuffs
> to do them, making their own whiskey and
> wine to drink, raising big families of
> children, living their own lives close to
> the soil. So I'm asking you why educate
> them?[24]

Coming from a man who has devoted so much of
his life to education, these words show Stuart at
his lowest ebb, close to despair over the exploit-
ative bigotry that continually threatens his beloved Appalachian way of life. But for all the
odds against them, despair is very uncommon in
Stuart and among his Appalachians. The personalized
loyalties and independence fostered by Appalachian
culture coupled with the relentless pressure exerted
by the world outside the mountains have created a
race of fighters. Appalachians have always been
first in the nation's wars, and they are equally
dedicated to defending their traditional way of life
against all comers.

The Appalachian subculture is in the ironic position of conducting a double defense system. In time of war Appalachians have put aside their mattocks, mule plows and tractors to join members of the dominant culture in the defense of the nation; following the traditional armistice, Appalachians return to the hills to defend their way of life in the war against the dominant culture's pressure.

An awareness of the historical role of the Appalachian as an American soldier is necessary in understanding why he has fought so doggedly and successfully in the war against the dominant culture. No other American subculture has fought so gallantly for all Americans in time of the nation's need as the Appalachian people. One reason they are such avid patriots is that they have so often received the folded Stars and Stripes to place beside the picture of a smiling boy on the mantelpiece.

At the battle of Kings Mountain (1780), British Commander Major Patrick Ferguson called the Appalachian frontiersmen "barbarians." In this battle 1104 British officers and men were killed or captured and 28 "barbarians" died. The dread Rebel Yell of the Civil War was learned by Appalachian soldiers from their forefathers, who learned it from Indian warriors. Appalachian soldiers of both the North and the South hated the regimen of the Army. Still, in the war with Spain (1898) and in the First World War (1917), so many Kentuckians from Breathitt County volunteered that it was "the only county in the United States in which the draft never became operative." Some Kentucky volunteers walked one hundred and seventy miles to "join up" at Lexington, Kentucky.[25] Jesse Stuart's family has been represented in every American campaign from the Revolutionary War to Viet Nam and this is a typical Appalachian record.

Stuart's proud Appalachians gladly give their life's blood in defense of the American people. In sonnets 584-587 of <u>Man With A Bull-Tongue Plow</u>, brothers Jacob and John Kouns die at the battle of Cold Harbor in the Civil War. The Kentucky father of sonnet 82 will give his "tall sons" when the

Country needs fighting men: "No matter if they're left to sleep full sound!" In Album of Destiny Cremeans Bentley calls upon his brothers to help him defend America. He tells them it is time for the mountain clans to fight in the nations's war. His call to battle has overtones that run throughout English poetry and reach all the way back to Beowulf:

> We must be rid of dangerous enemies,
> Strike at the tyrants with a broadax stroke.

In sonnet 535 (M W B-T P) Bill Tong's body is returned from France "wrapped in Old Glory." Bill's strong lungs were riddled by machine gun bullets near the River Marne. Stuart's Appalachian men of war emerge as cultural heroes in their willingness to suffer and die for their country's needs. Stuart lauds this disinterested largess in the Appalachian ethos and damns those petty war scavengers who exploit it for their own selfish ends. The persona of sonnet 333 (M W B-T P) conducts the annual Appalachian Memorial Day rite of cleaning and decorating the graves of kinfolk--particularly those hillmen who have died in the nation's wars. The persona sheds warm tears for these mountain dead but curses those lesser men who manipulated them:

> Now what to hell was marching to a fife,
> And what to hell was marching to a drum,
> Marching out to give a life or take a life--
> Just stepping proudly to a fife and drum!
> You rest: Commercial war gods did their
> best.

"The War and Cousin Lum" and "Beyond the News in Still Hollow" are two Stuart short stories that celebrate this disinterested bravery of the Appalachian subculture. Cousin Lum returns home following World War I with one eye and half of one foot. He declares that he won't serve his final six days in the army unless there is another war.[26] Sheriff Eric Bradley of Melton County worries about traveling into the remoteness of Still Hollow to capture the supposed World War II draft dodger, Crooks Cornett. Sheriff Bradley is warmly received by the Cornett family who have never heard of World

War II. They give him lodging for the night, feed
him a sumptuous supper and breakfast, and their
youngest son is heartbroken because he cannot accompany Crooks, his older brother to help fight the
war. The Cornetts proudly show the sheriff their
family Bible; it carries the inscription "Yorkshire,
England, May 17th, 1797."[27]

Jesse Stuart's patriotic hillmen fight an equally
courageous battle in defense of their Appalachian
subculture and in defiance of the dominant culture's
increasing pressure for change. Stuart has unflinch-
ingly spoken for the right of the Appalachian people
to continue their culture: "Appalachia will not be
destroyed. . . . England for nearly 2,000 years has
remained England; Scotland has remained Scotland;
Wales has remained Wales and Ireland has remained
Ireland. Appalachia remains Appalachia."[28] Stuart
has both stated and shown that the Appalachian culture is exactly that--a culture--and as such it has
a right to exist: "Appalachia has a culture of its
own and what makes it such a great place in which
to live and write about is the fact that Appalachia
has dared to retain this culture, defying pressure
by outside areas to conform."[29]

As we have seen, the lines of conflict between
the dominant American culture and the Appalachian
subculture are firmly drawn in Stuart's work and
the Appalachian often gives as well as he gets:

I get so damned tired of pretty politeness
From sissy men in small-town soda fountains;
Maybe they equally despise the ruggedness
And sturdiness of the men from the mountains.[30]

To the dominant culture's charge that the Appalachian lacks the years of formal education of his
"cultural better" the persona of sonnet 394 (M W
B-T P) answers that even though hill men are referred to as children of the night because they
cannot read or write, they know many things and
possess much wisdom not found in books. The persona
of sonnet 690 cannot tolerate Ph.D.'s who act like
Ph.D.'s:

Oh, it is strange how people run a bluff

23

And put themselves above the things they are.
They look upon unlettered men with scoff,
Those chosen intellectuals striving for
To drop ten pole-beans down a craw-dad hole
And give to charity--God bless their souls!

The persona-writer of sonnets 655-659 declares his
independence of the dominant culture's tea-circle
school of polite poetry by stating that he does not
belong to literary cliques or clans and that he is
"unafraid to gut and bone."

In God's Oddling Stuart relates his unsuccess-
ful attempt to build a new home, complete with all
the modern conveniences, for his hardworking farm
parents, Mick and Sal (Mitchell and Martha Hilton
Stuart). In typical Appalachian fashion they
quickly and politely inform their son that they
will remain in their modest frame house--a home
filled with precious memories.[31] In The Year of
My Rebirth, Stuart says that no man should ever
pity hillmen of his generation because these men
had the privilege of growing up in a world that
gave one time to think--a time when a man with the
fastest fox hounds was as highly admired as a successful businessman is today.[32]

This refusal of the Appalachian subculture to
adopt the status interpretation of the dominant
culture is explicit in Stuart's short story "Pockets
Full of North Wind." The story's fox hunters are
not cowed by the symbolic presence of the dominant
culture as they race two miles down hill to beat a
train to a crossing. They think of themselves as
hounds and the train as the fox, and they give it
everything they've got to "beat er"--the last man
across has his coat tails brushed by the engine of
a shouting engineer.[33]

In the introduction to Yesterday's People,
Robert B. Vance truly states that ". . . the crux
of the problem is clear. To change the mountains
is to change the mountain personality." Long before and after Yesterday's People the potential for
Appalachian cultural death has been a major theme
spanning the entire literary production of Jesse
Stuart. For the Appalachian to yield completely

to the relentless pressure of the dominant culture
is for him to go the way of his earliest tutor for
survival in his highland home--the American Indian.

In Album of Destiny Fain Groan, speaking to his
son, could well be the embodiment of the Appalachian
ethos advising her sons to remain home or, if they
have to go away to work, to at least return home
for periodic renewals of their souls:

Too long away from what fox-eyes discern,
Will leave you like the dead oaks on these hills
. . . .
My son, return to land of whipporwills
And rain-drenched misty hills where you were
born. (40)

Even the mountain copperhead of Album longs for the
cool recesses by his home stream. He hates the man
who put him in a cage and bites his jailor at the
first opportunity (145).

Since the early years of his career, Stuart has
been highly aware of the homogeneity, the homing
instinct and the resistance to outside cultural
pressure of his Appalachian subculture: "The dialect we speak is quite different to that of any
region in America. . . . It is our own. I can almost tell a mountaineer's voice as soon as I hear
him speak. If I couldn't tell him by his dialect,
I would know him by his idiom of speech. I think
his language is more musical than any other dialect
spoken in America. Many of the words in our vocab-
ularies go back to Chaucerian English. You will
find 'archaic' Shakespearean English still spoken
by Appalachian mountaineers, and our 'hillbilly'
country, to those of us who have lived in the
mountains, no matter where we travel, is still the
most beautiful in the world."[34]

In the short story "W-Hollow Man" Stuart presents an insight into the stand-off battle of acculturation through the ultimate "regression" of a
seemingly acculturated Appalachian. Hill man
Brasque Maynard, who married the beautiful town
girl Edith Mae Wampler and moved to Blakesburg, is
dying of cancer, and he wants to visit W-Hollow in

25

its four seasons during the remaining year of his
life. His wife doesn't understand why he wants to
return to the mountains, hear the hoot owls, and
watch wild deer grazing on honeysuckle vines in
winter:

> "Well, I was born in W-Hollow and I
> grew up there and it's not only home but
> it's Heaven to me," he said. . . . "Five
> miles from here, for old Brasq, has been
> the difference in Heaven and Hell. I had
> to tell you this dearest one; it's too late
> for me to sit in this bed and lie to you
> now." . . . .
> "I'll die in Blakesburg, in this house,
> in this bed, but I'll die a W-Hollow man
> with all the sights and sounds and images
> I got from W-Hollow embedded in my heart
> and brain. Three generations of W-Hollow
> ancestors made me what I am."[35]

The Appalachian subculture that can inspire
such love is under unrelenting pressure for change
by the dominant American culture: "The forces of
change are under way and, no doubt, will pick up
speed as the next few years pass. The folk culture
is under tremendous pressure to change--yes, even
to pass out of existence, for those who work in
Appalachia, not understanding the values of the
culture, will try to destroy the folk customs and
the culture and force the Southern highlander into
the conforming mode of the rest of America."[36]

Valiant as Appalachia's struggle for cultural
independence has been, it has been piecemeal.
Many sociologists have maintained that the one
thing lacking is a concept of Appalachian nation-
alism, a concept which has just recently begun to
emerge and is the hope for the future.[37] As the
greatest literary spokesman of the Appalachian
subculture, Jesse Stuart has been defining and
calling for Appalachian cultural unity throughout
his lifetime:

> Westward past the sloping watershed of
> Virginia and Carolina; south of the Ohio,
> the Kanawha, the Greenbrier; east of the

26

Kentucky and Tennessee blue grass; north
of Atlanta and northeast of Birmingham:
These lands, these crested Appalachians,
are home for four million people with a
tradition born in the spawning of Anglo-
Saxon-Celtic history and matured in the
American highlands.

It is a proud land; we are a proud
people. It is a rugged and individualistic and loving land; so are the people.

Despite mass communications, and with
good roads up the valleys and over the
mountains, the highlanders hold to old
traditions more than any other segment of
the national population. We remain the
least changed--holdouts against an American mass culture--with one of the most
stable, sturdy, and stubborn peoples in
the nation. Our geographical, ancestral,
and cultural roots bind us together as a
small, fiercely loyal country within a
country.[38]

It is a unique feature of Stuart's literary
career that he has been not only the most profound
authority on his subculture but one of its strongest defenders. He feels that too many of his
fellow Appalachians have succumbed to the unrelenting pressure of the dominant culture and have
mistakenly moved out of Appalachia, which the
dominant culture defines as a poor country: "They
call this a poor, blighted, Appalachian land but
I call it the most beautiful, the most fruitful,
the greatest place on earth. Somebody has to be
wrong."[39]

The dominant-culture assumption that, given
sufficient exposure, the Appalachian will naturally
choose the "superior" way of life of the American
mass culture is a fallacy. For Jesse Stuart and
the Appalachian ethos, nothing could be further
from the truth. The bland mass-media T.V. world
of young, ulcerated executives--that world where
no one is responsible for anything nor can possibly
solve his own problems--is a veritable living Hell
to the Appalachian. Its frightening anonymity and
often Kafkaesque absurdity is a refutation of the

Appalachian's most deeply held beliefs about himself and about the nature of man.

For Jesse Stuart and the Appalachian ethos,
to lose the war of acculturation is to lose life
itself:

If I could now come back I would not come,
For my Kentucky hills have made a change.
The hill-man's heart stirs not to fife
and drum;
His hunting grounds have grown to something
strange.
It is all strange--white boards replace
the black.
There is no cutter plow nor hunting horn.
Nor farewell-summers growing near the shack;
There are no morning glories in the corn.
The Showmen cried: "The hills-men need
a change.
We'll send their young to school and iron
them out."
And if they need a change they got a change
To strawlings that the wind could blow about.
When their good work was done, our life was
lost.
And now men are the same from coast to coast.[40]

NOTES

1. Jesse Stuart, "Ascend the High Mountain,"
    Country Beautiful, Feb. 1962, pp. 13,14.

2. Jesse Stuart, "Kentucky," Kentucky Progress
    Magazine, 6 (Winter 1935), 256.

3. Jesse Stuart, "A Land and Its People," Register
    of the Kentucky Historical Society, 68 (July
    1970), 221, 222.

4. Jack E. Weller, Yesterday's People (Lexington,
    Ky.: University of Kentucky Press, 1965), pp.
    58-81, 59.

5. Jesse Stuart, Taps for Private Tussie (New York:
    The World Publishing Company, 1969), p. 283.

6. Jesse Stuart, Clearing in the Sky (New York:
    McGraw-Hill, 1950), pp. 118-132.

7. Jesse Stuart, My Land Has A Voice (New York:
    McGraw-Hill, 1966), pp. 185-196.

8. Jesse Stuart, "How to Thread a Needle," The
    Ohio University Review, IX (1967), 21.

9. Jesse Stuart, Man With a Bull-Tongue Plow
    (New York: E. P. Dutton, 1934), p. 20.

10. Jesse Stuart, Beyond Dark Hills (New York:
    E. P. Dutton, 1938), p. 54.

11. Jesse Stuart, Hie to the Hunters, (New York:
    McGraw-Hill, 1950), p. 88.

12. Jesse Stuart, Album of Destiny (New York:
    E. P. Dutton, 1944), p. 148.

13. Stuart, Clearing in the Sky, pp. 185-190.

14. Jesse Stuart, A Jesse Stuart Reader (New York:
    McGraw-Hill, 1963), pp. 121-129.

15. Jesse Stuart, Kentucky Is My Land (New York: E. P. Dutton, 1952), p. 15

16. Don West, "Romantic Appalachia," in Appalachia in the Sixties, ed. by David S. Walls and John B. Stephenson (Lexington, Ky.: University Press of Kentucky, 1972), p. 212.

17. Stuart, Album of Destiny, p. 224.

18. Ibid., 246.

19. Stuart, Clearing in the Sky, p. 216.

20. Jesse Stuart, The Good Spirit of Laurel Ridge (New York: McGraw-Hill, 1953), p. 53.

21. Stuart, Taps for Private Tussie, pp. 51-52.

22. Jesse Stuart, Come Back to the Farm (New York: McGraw-Hill, 1971), p. 8.

23. Jesse Stuart, The Land Beyond the River (New York: McGraw-Hill, 1973), pp. 313-314.

24. Jesse Stuart, "Leave The Mountaineers Alone?" New Republic, 9 May 1934, p. 366.

25. Harry M. Caudill, Night Comes to the Cumberlands, (Boston: Little, Brown, 1962), pp. 12, 39, 91.

26. Jesse Stuart, Come Gentle Spring (New York: McGraw-Hill, 1969), pp. 270-271.

27. Stuart, My Land Has a Voice, pp. 28-38.

28. Jesse Stuart, untitled article, Morgantown (W. Va.) Dominion News, 25 Feb. 1967, Sect. 2, p. 3.

29. Sandra Deeley, "Stuart Praises Appalachia," Morgantown (W. Va.) Daily Athenaeum, 28 Feb. 1967, No. 84. p. 1.

30. Stuart, Man With a Bull-Tongue Plow, p. 203.

31. Jesse Stuart, God's Oddling (New York: McGraw-Hill, 1960), p. 232.

32. Jesse Stuart,.The Year of My Rebirth (New York: McGraw-Hill, 1956), pp. 282-283.

33. Jesse Stuart, "Pockets Full of North Wind," in Kentucky Writing, ed. by James McConkey (Morehead, Ky.: Morehead State College, 1954), pp. 43-55.

34. Jesse Stuart, "We 'Hillbillies'," Pageant, March 1945, p. 74.

35. Jesse Stuart, "W-Hollow Man," Arizona Quarterly, 24 (Summer 1968), 153, 157.

36. Weller, Yesterday's People, pp. 134-135.

37. David S. Walls and John B. Stephenson, eds., Appalachia in the Sixties (Lexington, Ky.: University Press of Kentucky, 1972), XV.

38. Stuart, "Ascend the High Mountain," p. 9.

39. Jesse Stuart, "Straths in the Green Valley Below," American Forests, Aug. 1968, p. 54.

40. Stuart, Man With a Bull-Tongue Plow, p. 350.

Jesse Stuart with the bull-tongue plow

CHAPTER TWO

SUBSISTENCE AND EXPLOITATION OF RESOURCES

An Appalachian farm is more than a
place to live. It is a way of life.
It is a dream, a shrine, a shield
against tomorrow's uncertainties, a
fortress against the onslaught of modern technology.
At the same time, it can be a grim
place, a place of unrelenting super-
stitions, twisted life styles, deca-
dence and madness, amplified by the
loneliness and isolation of the ever-
present hills.[1]

To understand Jesse Stuart's painfully honest
embodiment of the means of subsistence in the
Appalachian subculture, it is necessary to know
how radically the economic history of Appalachia
differs from that of the rest of the United States.
As Dr. Earl Brewer has truly noted, the economics
of modern Appalachia is a hodgepodge and an anach-
ronism: "Where else can one find such contrasts
as Elizabethan folklore and atomic reactors,
planting by the moon and scientific agriculture,
medieval demonology and modern medicine, beliefs
that God sends floods to wipe out the sinful as
in Noah's time and TVA, the primitive Protestant
emphasis on individualism and the overloaded welfare rolls?"[2]

No other American author has even approached
Stuart in embodying the economic plight and outlook of so many of the nation's people in such a
large area: an area 600 miles in length, approximately 250 miles in width, consisting of nine
states, and with a population of approximately
eight million people.

The prototype of Jesse Stuart's Kentucky
mountaineers was already established in his wilderness by the time of the American Revolution.

His ancestors had been peasants and yeomen in
England, Scotland and Ireland. His fellow mountaineers were freedom-loving men who had left the
established colonial settlements and traveled
westward to real independence. Contrary to popular stereotypes, these early mountain settlers
"were not inspired Europeans determined to cross
the dangerous oceans and found a citadel of religious and economic freedom in the new world. They
were native North Americans with deeply engrained
mores, habits, and social outlook. The Kentucky
mountaineer, as a type, was already thoroughly
established. He had simply moved over a few hundred miles to find unplowed creek bottoms, a more
plentiful supply of game and to get away from his
neighbors."3

These independent Scotch Irishmen who dwell
among the dark hills of Jesse Stuart's vision have
suffered four "rediscoveries" by their American
brothers of the dominant culture. The first rediscovery of Appalachia was literary and lasted
roughly from 1870-1910. There was great national
interest in novels based on Appalachia with its
"quaint customs and dialect." For instance, John
Fox Jr. (a non-Appalachian who visited the mountains to get the dialect and customs right) became
very popular with his The Little Shepherd of King-
dom Come (1913) and The Trail of the Lonesome Pine
(1908).

The second rediscovery of Appalachia occurred
from 1895-1925 when the conscience of the nation
was aroused to the problems of the area by such
persons as Dr. William G. Frost, President of
Berea College, who was sponsored by the major
Protestant denominations.

During the early thirties Appalachians were
again rediscovered and "adopted" by outland lib-
eral groups concerned with the plight of coal
miners during the painful years of emerging union-
ism and the "coal wars" between coal operators and
organizing miners. The American novelist Theodore
Dreiser, one of the founders of the National Com-
mittee for the Defense of Political Prisoners, was
involved in this rediscovery. Other than gaining

brief national attention in newspapers, this movement did little to alter the lot of coal miners.

The fourth rediscovery of Appalachia began in the 1960's and involved President John F. Kennedy, Attorney General Robert Kennedy and President Lyndon B. Johnson--all of whom made televised visits "across the branch" to speak to their fellow Americans who inhabit the oldest frontier remaining in America. This latest rediscovery awakened a new national interest in Appalachia and its problems of "misery, ignorance and poverty."[4]

However, despite occasional good intentions, the dominant American culture has had a tragic impact upon the traditional means of subsistence in the Appalachain subculture: many of Stuart's unforgettable characters are living embodiments of this tragedy. Appalachia's self-sustaining farm way of life came under attack by non-Appalachian exploitation in the early nineteenth century and has continued to be assaulted until the present. The exploitation of Appalachia and her people has not been pretty either in its effect on Appalachian means of subsistence or in the irreversible alterations it has worked on the Appalachian way of life.

As Harry Caudill has noted in Night Comes to the Cumberlands, Appalachia first came under economic attack during the first quarter of the nineteenth century, when the Appalachian mountaineer was offered gold by outside timber companies for his beautifully straight virgin timber. The subsequent period of log rafting was the beginning of the road to a cash economy (35-36). The 1870's and 1880's saw the buying of tracts of virgin timber by Eastern businessmen and the building of railroads into the timber country of eastern Kentucky (61-65).

Following the mass slaughter of Appalachian timber, the second wave of eroding economic influence began in 1875 when personable land agents for Eastern and Northern coal companies started buying mineral rights at 26½ cents per acre in broad form deeds that gave coal companies all

minerals and the right to excavate by any means
possible--absolving the company from liability
for any damages done to the land owners (71-75)
⟨at this time, strip mining was unheard of⟩.
On the eve of World War I the Lexington and Eastern,
the Louisville and Nashville, and the Baltimore and
Ohio railroads built roads to tie the coal-rich
counties of eastern Kentucky to the industrial
complex of the North. This gave rise to a shift
of many mountaineers from their traditional hillside farms into the coal camps.

From the 1930's until the 1960's, additional
"plans" of the dominant culture for the economic
well-being of Appalachians spelled a virtual end
to the traditional Appalachian way of life. The
1930's and WPA saw the beginning of relief programs and a long process of demoralization for
the Appalachian (185). The 1950's witnessed welfarism, out-migration and strip mining (305).
The final blow to the traditional Appalachia came
by means of "legislative reform" in the 1960's.
The soil bank plan, developed to help farm prices
elsewhere, encouraged farmers of the Cumberland
plateau to let their mountain farms remain idle.
This ended the old Appalachain form of agriculture
based on mules, cornfields and domestic animals
(346).

Today's means of subsistence in Appalachia is
twofold: The Appalachian must supplement his
small farm way of life by commuting many miles to
jobs primarily in coal fields and large industrial
cities, or he must join the welfare roles. Many
mountaineers have been forced to leave their homeland to earn a decent living for their families.
Still others, having been mercilessly exploited
in all their major economic contacts with the dominant culture for generations, have adopted some
regional attitudes that are incomprehensible to
many outside the subculture: "Materialism has
brought them suffering and destitution and they
lack spiritual values to support them in their
distress. Mingled with this spiritual emptiness
and immensely aggravating it is the awareness of
futility and ineffectiveness that besets the unskilled in a highly technical and complex world.

36

Out of this background has grown a mass melancholia
of ominous and ever-deepening proportions. To escape its grip some commit suicide while others, in
numbers we can only guess at, find surcease in the
cheap product of tiny household stills" (350).

Throughout his long and highly successful literary career, Jesse Stuart has been aware of the
shameful exploitation of Appalachian resources and
the irreversible impact of that exploitation upon
the lives of Appalachians and their particular
means of subsistence: "Appalachia is anywhere
there is coal under the ground. There are different states and worlds inside it, but we're all
bound together by that one thing--coal. . . .
Long before the eloquent prose of Harry Caudill,
long before the Peace Corps and poverty programs,
long before the outsiders discovered the tie-dye
fabrics and mountain crafts at Berea College, this
65-year-old writer was expounding the beauties,
tragedies and mordant humor of the region."[5]

Stuart's Appalachians have traditionally sup-
ported their families through a combination of
small hillside farming and unskilled labor jobs.
When Stuart was born in Greenup County, Kentucky,
in 1907, few hillmen worked for industry; they
farmed and hunted a wild, unpolluted country, and
depended on domestic animals for a large portion
of their livelihood.[6] By the 1940's most hillmen
had sold their mineral and timber rights and many
had lost their land as the freedom and independence
of life-sustaining mountain farms were rapidly
disappearing.[7] Both the early independent Appalachian way of life and the later exploited Appalachia are depicted throughout Stuart's works,
and those works make it clear that the passing of
the old way of life has not necessarily resulted
in an easier one.

When Jesse Stuart burst upon the literary scene
in 1934, writing about the common people, the reaction of many members of the dominant culture to
this self-announced poet of mountain people was one
of cultural shock. In sonnet 3 of Man With A Bull-
Tongue Plow, the young poet announced his intention
to sing of the men and land he had known--a land of

crows, hawks, and toiling men plowing rugged soil:

> Better to sing of life from where I start--
> From mountain folks and from Kentucky hills.
> Better to sing and never ask a dime
> For ruggedness I spin into a rhyme,
> For I can live--to hell with all your gold.[8]

One major theme running throughout this great book is the inner beauty of mountain people who work to support their families in a rugged land. Sonnet 49 praises the beauty of a mountain mother who has done more than her share of work without complaint. Great strength of character emanates from the lines:

> The tree in you, flower in you, the hill,
> Color of autumn leaf, the twisted grape-vine
> will. (27)

This hard working mountain mother still possesses the power to love "a child, a stone, a star." Sonnets 51 and 52 praise the equal strength of a mountain father--a man who has lived a life of work and loves his animals and the soil: "He's of the dirt and he'll go back to dirt."

Throughout Man With A Bull-Tongue Plow, there are sonnets dealing with the economic exploitation of Appalachia: sonnets 73, 93, and 264 are typical. In sonnet 73, Bert Skaggs says that big men take his tobacco crop by extending him reduced credit for its full value. Ike Mullins, sonnet 93, cut millions of trees for lumber companies when he was a strong young man; he has grown old with little to show for his labor. In sonnet 264 the persona is a man who cuts cross-ties for $1.20 a day in order to help feed his wife and ten children.

During October of 1934 Stuart published a letter in The New Republic which provides an insight into his feelings regarding the exploitation of Appalachian resources:

> . . . Now about what Mr. Cowley was saying
> in his review /of Paul Engle's American
> Song7 about the country being exploited

(by the spirit of pioneer individualism that Engle glorified). I wish Paul Engle could only take a look at this part of Kentucky, at the hills where no plow can ever furrow and where the trees are all gone. The coal is all gone; nothing is left but the old sprouty hills. I say our section of Kentucky has been exploited. Where the old coal banks used to be, a yellow blood (sulphur water) oozes from the gutted hills. I get so mad at times I could cry. It does me a hell of a lot of good. I have seen in my life every hard foot of road to Greenup County, and I have seen all the timber in my vicinity disappear. Paul Engle has not seen this.[9]

In Beyond Dark Hills Stuart portrays the livelihoods of three generations of Appalachia. There is grandfather Mitchell Stuart, the living embodiment of the old way of life in Appalachia before the economic impact of the twentieth century. Grandpa Mitch emerges as a giant of the Big Sandy country: he was a prosperous farmer and timberman who could outwork any man. He was the "fightin Stuart," so feisty that his fellow union soldiers once hanged him by the thumbs to calm him down.

Secondly, there are Jesse's father, 'Little Mitch,' and his mother, Martha Hilton—two hard-working mountain parents who were tenants on a series of places before buying their first farm when Jesse was a young man. Jesse's parents worked hard on hillside farms to support a family of five children /two other children died at a young age/ who themselves worked in the fields helping their parents. Jesse's father also worked in small coal mines during the winter months to supplement the family income, and for many years he worked as a section hand on the railroad—often doing his farm chores in the darkness of early morning and night in order to pay for his fifty-acre hillside farm.

Thirdly, there is the life of the twentieth-century Appalachian, Jesse Stuart. As a young boy, Jesse learned the feel of the bull-tongue plow pulled by a team of mules—often from daylight

39

until dark. We see him working at paving the streets of Greenup, Kentucky, before deciding to enter the beautiful high school there. Following graduation, young Jesse was dissatisfied with the routine of hill work and decided to work for a street carnival which fired him for giving free rides to the boys and girls.

At the age of 18 Jesse went to work as a laborer in the Armco Steel mill at Ashland, Kentucky, and on September 12, 1926, he quit his job there, paid off a $300 debt, and set out, with a total savings of $29.30, to find himself a college. He put himself through Lincoln Memorial University in Harrogate, Tennessee, by working on the college farm—digging water lines, laying bricks, cutting corn, and so forth. Later, he attended Vanderbilt University for his graduate work where he worked seven hours a day as a janitor in addition to his graduate studies in English.

The old Appalachian proverb that 'a man who can make a living in the hills can make a living on a rock' is nowhere better illustrated than in Stuart's writings. Mick, Sal, Shan, Finn, and the Powderjay girls work incessantly throughout Stuart's writing, as the Stuart family have done in real life. Fronnie Bushman, in Trees of Heaven, truly maintains that the two kinds of hill people are those who starve and those who work themselves to death;[10] and many characters in Stuart's short stories suffer these fates.

"Uncle Jeff" is the story of Mick, Shan, and Finn Powderjay's trip to Ferton, West Virginia, on a last visit to uncle Jeff—a man who has worked himself to death as a section hand on the railroad.[11] "Vacation in Hell" is an even more tragic story of two young men who supplement the farm income during the winter months by crawling into a shaft mine and picking coal all day for 5¢ per bushel. Both men support large families and consider the work a vacation in hell—where scampering rats often indicate a cave-in. One of the men is killed in a slate fall and the other is permanently crippled.[12]

The exploitation of Appalachian resources and human lives is vividly mirrored in Stuart's works, especially the impact of the great lumber and coal mining interests which have had the biggest hand in the process and the most destructive influence on the traditional Appalachian family system. Sid Seagraves of Taps for Private Tussie and the Boliver Tussie family of Trees of Heaven are but two of Stuart's characters who suffer in a peculiarly Appalachian sense. Sid's father, the son of a coal operator, refused to marry Sid's mother, a coal miner's daughter. The Boliver Tussies, a family of timber cutters, could not afford to buy the land they had lived on for years from the lumber company and became tenants on their own property. In The Good Spirit of Laurel Ridge Theopolis Akers lives on the ridge because he loves it and remembers the Big Sandy country of an earlier day of big timber, iron ore and charcoal. In contrast to those prosperous times, Theopolis now lives off the land and makes spending money by selling nuts and berries in Honeywell.

Contrary to popular stereotypes, the economic wonder of Stuart's Appalachia is not that so many receive welfare benefits but that so many unrecognized and unapplauded hillmen and their families fight so desperately to survive independently in a world of tax shelters. Like Uncle Thorny Kirk in "The Best Years of Our Lives," many have difficulty in ascertaining the sanity of a culture that pays certain men not to produce anything on farms that businessmen feel compelled to fly over in jets at speeds fast enough to crack the roof and ceiling.[13]

Further complicating the problem of subsistence in the Appalachian subculture and in Stuart's depiction of it is the fact (unknown or often overlooked by members of the dominant culture) that the Appalachian has a work ethic all his own. The Appalachian works in order to live rather than living in order to work. Because of his harsh environment the Appalachian does not share the "progressive" life view of most Americans. Unlike middle class Americans, the Appalachian does not view new cars, bigger homes, and more cultural opportunities as being vital to a better life.[14] Stuart's Battle

Keaton, an old man who has poured his sweat and blood into his bare hill acres, looks at the bushes retaking his farm and wonders what the work of man amounts to. He requests that he be buried in a blue work shirt and his underwear.[15]

In Album of Destiny Jesse Stuart presents many classic portraits of hardworking Appalachians who, unlike most modern laborers, question the meaning of human existence and their labors upon this earth. They are Americans who have not become cogs in the machine and who would die rather than become depersonalized automatons of any system of production. Sebie Nelson asks if the life of mountain men who take time from work to smell a blue corn-flower and watch a passing cloud has been in vain.

Wilson Smack is glad to be working before dawn in autumn fields of hay and corn in order to feed his family of ten. The smell of wild fox grapes and the sight of "shoe-make antlers" in the fence rows are treasured by this farmer who misses these sights and sounds of nature in his other job as coal miner:

> I know not night nor day in this dark hole;
> I know the powder, pick, the fork and bar,
> The touch of earth, a helpless-handed mole;
> My eyes don't see the beauty of a star.[16]

In like manner, Mace Bushman has the memories of laboring in the steel mill as a youth etched indelibly upon his brain:

> Those days are colorless as furnace slag . . .
> Ten hours each day, and lodgings were unclean.
> The pencil marks of blood and steel and sweat
> Are in my veins . . . I know I can't forget. (88)

At the end of their lives of hard work, Jesse Stuart's mountain dead are "good seeds planted beneath the briar, the rose, dirt, wind and sky" (182).

In Come Back to the Farm, 91-year-old Cass Timberlake and his wife Bridget wonder if there is any new ground left to plow in their section

of Appalachia. They have moved once in order to
avoid the dominant culture: they do not like the
busy traffic on roads created by steel monsters.
They mourn the fact that young men of the area no
longer work hard as their forefathers did to farm
the hilly land; these young Appalachians plow only
the flat valley land and ride tractors to do that.[17]

The traditional Appalachian farming way of life
had been destroyed by the late 1940's, and countless Appalachians began the process of migration
to the outland labor market. The years 1948-1960
saw one of the greatest and least publicized mass
migrations in American history. There was a vast
loss of population from the Cumberlands to Ohio,
Indiana and Michigan because king coal was seriously ill in Appalachia. Small coal operators were
going bankrupt by the hundreds, and thousands of
miners were out of work. Amazingly, the Appalachian
family system held together during the migrations
of so many Appalachians to the large northern
industrial cities:

> Now, the family not only performs the
> function of telling potential migrants
> at home about jobs and getting them out
> there but educates and socializes them
> after they arrive so that they learn
> how to behave in this greater society.
> . . . .
> This is one reason we don't hear so ter-
> ribly much about this great migration
> which, in scope, dwarfs a lot of the
> movements of people we do hear a whole
> lot about. It is amazing how fast the
> migration can be turned off if there
> aren't jobs out in the Midwestern cities.
> Family members pass the word back home,
> and migration is delayed until times get
> better.[18]

In the outland labor market the Appalachian,
although known there as the hardest of workers,
is not always a resounding success as is indicated
by the Appalachian ghettoes and "hillbilly bars"
of Cleveland, Detroit and Chicago. The problems
of adjustment of Appalachians in "Uptown," a Chicago

ghetto, are typical:

> Of the many ethnic groups that make up America's cities, few experience the difficulty in becoming "urbanized" that besets the migrant Southerner. In the city, virtually every principle of his life becomes a rural value struggling to retain its identity against an urban value that demands precedence. It is a cultural struggle: the personal against the impersonal, independence against regimentation. It is the casual laborer learning that in the city jobs do not wait for those who do not report to them every day. It is the fear and distrust of the formal, signed paper society of the city; a man must sign a lease to rent a good apartment, a mortgage to own a home. . . . .
> In the end, the Southerner has only exchanged the open-space poverty of the rural South for the ghetto poverty of the northern city. Whether or not he ever adjusts to urban life depends largely on his own endurance and how much help he can find along the way.
> Those who experience the most difficulty in adjusting are the Appalachians. For more so than any other present-day ethnic group in America, the Appalachian seems to consider home to be where the heart is, and no matter where he might go the Appalachian nearly always leaves his heart behind in the hills.[19]

Many of Jesse Stuart's Appalachians return to quench their thirst for the "lonesome waters" of their mountain home. They return across the Ohio River in endless streams of traffic on every major holiday, and on Memorial Day weekend they decorate the graves of their mountain dead. They recross the big river late on Sunday nights and travel sleepy-eyed to distant northern cities to begin a weary Monday workday. The vast majority would return home immediately if attractive jobs existed in Appalachia. The reason that Appalachia has no

44

skilled labor force is that force is living and
working in large northern cities--a fact that politicians slyly ignore. Most Appalachians return
home to be buried, and one great theme running
throughout the works of Jesse Stuart is his lyrical
descriptions of the feeling of Appalachians for the
hills of home. They are beyond question some of
the most powerful descriptions in American literature of the deep emotional ties between Americans
and their homeland, and they rank squarely with
Henry David Thoreau's similar descriptions in
Walden Pond:

> Born in W-Hollow, you may leave for a
> time but will return to live and die
> in W-Hollow. . . . .
> There is something to W-Hollow, maybe
> the sound of lonesome waters purring
> and singing day and night, perhaps
> the sounds of lonesome winds singing
> in all four seasons up and down the
> valley, and, maybe the invisible shapes
> of those gone before still on the wind
> are the things that call them back to
> live and die in W-Hollow.[20]

It is this cherished Appalachia that has witnessed "the most staggering destruction of land
and water in the history of the nation;" unfortu-
nately, several additional economic factors have
led to further impoverishment of its people.[21]
A welfare state which is politically administered
and is a powerful political force in all of Appalachia began in the Great Depression of the 1930's
with relief programs and initiated the long process
of demoralization for many mountaineers. And the
1950's further darkened the economic picture for
these Appalachians when the strengthening of Welfarism coincided with the great out migration of
Appalachian laborers and the introduction of strip
mining into the area.[22]

The 1960's witnessed further miscarriages of
programs designed by the dominant culture to aid
the depressed areas of Appalachia. In 1961 the
Establishment of the Area Redevelopment Adminis-
tration, a private industry incentive effort, failed.

The Economic Act of 1964, consisting of public and community action programs and food stamps--although intended to help, and in fact helping some indigent Appalachians--has demoralized many Appalachians by removing the incentive to work. Finally, The Appalachian Regional Development Act of 1965--an attempt to funnel federal aid through local districts detached from local political control--has succeeded chiefly in making Appalachian politicians and their allies more wealthy.[23]

Jesse Stuart has always been an arch foe of the Appalachian welfare system because of what it has done to the pride of those mountain folk who receive welfare. He has written two masterful satires directed against the mountain welfare system, not against folks who receive welfare: Taps for Private Tussie (1943) and The Land Beyond the River (1973).

For a time in Taps for Private Tussie, Grandpa Tussie, and his family lead the comfortable life of the dominant culture on the $10,000 insurance money received from the government for Private Kim Tussie's death in battle. They live well but not too wisely and lay waste their wealth by renting a sixteen-room mansion where they are soon descended upon by forty of their non-welfare Tussie clan who are determined to live with Grandpa and square dance the night away until the money runs out. Because of them Grandpa and his immediate family of four are evicted from the mansion: Grandpa is terminated from the relief roles and must return to the harsh life in the hills--to a shack and fifty acres of land he has bought with the final $300 of his daughter-in-law's windfall. The final indignity comes when Grandpa discovers that because he has become a landowner for the first time in his life his old age pension is cancelled.

Revealing more abuses of the growing American welfare state is Stuart's Land Beyond the River. At the encouragement of a relative already working and living in Ohio, Gil and Sil Perkins decide to take their ten children, leave their Kentucky mountain home and move to the wonderful state of Ohio-- which has better job opportunities and higher Social Security, welfare, and old-age benefits. In Ohio,

the Perkins family receives a total monthly bene-
fit of $1500 and food stamps, free medical expenses,
free school lunches, free school breakfasts and free
college educations.

The flagrant abuses of the system are so ridiculous that by the end of the novel they have so much
excess cash that they plan to bank in other counties
in order to avoid suspicion. However, the oldest
Perkins son is looking forward with more than mere
anticipation to the opportunity of going to work at
the Dupont Chemical Plant. He is sick of the welfare system and wants nothing further to do with
such things as food stamps. He is anxious to work
for his daily bread as an American contributing to
America and restore the self-pride that was and is
such a cherished part of his proud Appalachian heritage.

NOTES

1. Dave Peyton, "The Appalachian Farm--As Jesse Stuart Sees It," review of Come Back to the Farm, by Jesse Stuart, in Huntington (W. Va.) Herald Advertiser, June 6, 1971.

2. Harry W. Ernst and Charles H. Drake, "The Lost Appalachians," in Appalachia in the Sixties, ed. by David S. Walls and John B. Stephenson (Lexington, Ky.: University Press of Kentucky, 1972), pp. 4-5.

3. Harry M. Caudill, Night Comes to the Cumberlands (Boston: Little, Brown, 1962), pp. 8-10.

4. Robert F. Munn, "The Latest Rediscovery of Appalachia," in Appalachia in the Sixties, pp. 26-30.

5. Betty Garrett, "An Appalachian Author Describes His Life Style," Appalachia, 6 (Dec. 1972-Jan. 1973), p. 25.

6. Jesse Stuart, Save Every Lamb (New York: McGraw-Hill, 1964), pp. 1-2.

7. Mary Washington Clarke, The Folklore of the Cumberlands as Reflected in the Writings of Jesse Stuart (Ann Arbor: University of Michigan Microfilms, Inc., 1960), p. 32.

8. Jesse Stuart, Man With A Bull-Tongue Plow (New York: E. P. Dutton, 1934), p. 12.

9. Jesse Stuart, Letter from Stuart to Editor, New Republic, LXX (Oct. 10, 1934), 1036.

10. Jesse Stuart, Trees of Heaven (New York: E. P. Dutton, 1940), p. 55.

11. Jesse Stuart, Head o' W-Hollow (New York: E. P. Dutton, 1936), p. 93.

12. Jesse Stuart, Men of the Mountains (New York: E. P. Dutton, 1941), pp. 266-282.

13. Jesse Stuart, <u>Come Back to the Farm</u> (New York: McGraw-Hill, 1971), p. 103.

14. Jack E. Weller, <u>Yesterday's People</u> (Lexington, Ky.: University of Kentucky Press, 1965), pp. 106, 35.

15. Jesse Stuart, <u>Tales From the Plum Grove Hills</u> (New York: E. P. Dutton, 1946), pp. 160-164.

16. Jesse Stuart, <u>Album of Destiny</u> (New York: E. P. Dutton, 1944), p. 110.

17. Stuart, <u>Come Back to the Farm</u>, p. 244.

18. James S. Brown, "The Family Behind The Migrant," in <u>Appalachia in the Sixties</u>, p. 154.

19. Bill Montgomery, "The Uptown Story," in <u>Appalachia in the Sixties</u>, pp. 144-145.

20. Jesse Stuart, "W-Hollow Man," <u>Arizona Quarterly</u>, 24 (Summer 1968), 147.

21. John Fetterman, "A Bold Idea for a New Appalachia," in <u>Appalachia in the Sixties</u>, p. 232.

22. Caudill, <u>Night Comes to the Cumberlands</u>, pp. 185-186, 305.

23. David S. Walls and John B. Stephenson, eds., <u>Appalachia in the Sixties</u>, xii-xiii.

Jesse Stuart with the two star characters of <u>Mongrel Mettle</u>--
Jerry B. Boneyard (left) and Trusty Red Rusty (right)

CHAPTER THREE

TEMPORALITY

One reason for the Appalachian's failure to be
completely assimilated by the dominant culture and
for Jesse Stuart having occasionally been criticized
for his development of time motif is a general lack
of understanding or willingness to permit the Appalachian concept of temporality. This concept is
very different from the clock-regulated, eight-hour
day, five-day-week, two-week-vacation-with-pay,
overtime with double pay of industrialized America:

> Time is ecological and structural--ecolog-
> ical in being based on man's response to
> changes in nature. It is structural in
> being a conceptualization of activities
> within a social group, primarily within
> the family. Time, thus, is not a thing
> that it is in most of American society.
> It is not something to be wasted or saved
> or cut into arbitrary units to which all
> events must then conform. Calendrical
> dates and chronometric hours which are
> all important to the outer society are
> unimportant in the neighborhood. Instead,
> there is a rhythm of changing activities
> in response to the succession of seasons
> and the life history of individuals and
> families. . . . Neighborhood life flows
> along in terms of changing situations and
> changing seasons. Work is accomplished
> in a setting of lifelong ties to kin and
> land, not by a rigid schedule of tasks
> that must be done at a certain time.[1]

Jesse Stuart's handling of the Appalachian time concept throughout his poetry, novels and short stories
is one of his great fortes as an artist, and com-
pares with William Faulkner's looping chronology
or Thomas Wolfe's time-negating lyricism.

Stuart's literary creations, as is true of living

51

Appalachians, cannot and will not accept the time
ethos of the dominant culture which defines time in
relation to money and, therefore, defines people's
lives in relation to money and things. In direct
contrast to the dominant culture's myth of perennial
youth , Stuart's Appalachians do not believe that
they are destined for physical immortality. Therefore, when they live, love, laugh, work, mediate,
drink and die, it is always against the awful and
swift passage of time.

      In sonnet 114 of M W B-T P the persona is a
young man in love walking with his beloved Jean in
springtime; as he walks he thinks that the swift
passage of time is like the drifting of white spring
cherry blossoms upon the wind. Similarly, in sonnet
526 the persona feels that man's life is as fleeting
as that of a petal that blooms only for a day. The
fact that lovers do come to dust is powerfully captured in sonnet 179, in which the initials cut in
beech trees have outlived the lovers who carved
them.

      It is this awareness of man's fleeting life
that makes the persona of sonnet 220 want to cease
hoeing corn on a beautiful summer day. He wants to
go rambling barefooted and hatless through the
beautiful hills and go swimming. He realizes that
some day corn will grow from his bosom. In sonnet
123 Stuart presents an image of man's fleeting life
that occurs on countless occasions in his work. It
is a deserted, decaying house--the family have gone,
and nature is reclaiming a man's home and land.

      It is this differing time concept and subse-
quent orientation to the universe that make the
personas of sonnets 242 and 292 unable to accept or
adjust to city life. In sonnet 242 the persona could
not adapt to the city and its ways; he tried but went
mad. Everything was grind, there was no music on
city streets and there was no place for a man to be
alone. The persona of sonnet 292 can find no comfort
in the cold stone city streets. His eyes can find
no visions in the "white blocks of city stones--and
dry electric fires," and he aches for the lonely
skies and night water--wind sounds of home.[2]

Many of the magnificent sonnets of M W B-T P derive their greatness from Stuart's ability to capture the timeless universality at the root of much Appalachian cultural activity; by so doing, Stuart achieves a still point in a turning world and links his Appalachia to the ages. One such sonnet is 141, which reveals the intimations of eternity behind an Appalachian foxhunt. This is the same time mystique found in Faulkner's symbolic and factual hunt in The Bear. Stuart's persona, on a cold clear March night of white moon, is listening to his foxhound in a chase:

> And on a frosted hill where white stars glisten,
> I stand chilled by the wind and listen, listen!

What the persona hears and what the reader hears are hound wailings carried on volleying currents of wind and bringing in the same eternal note of sadness that Sophocles heard on the Aegean and Matthew Arnold by the English Channel.

Many personas of Album of Destiny provide additional insight into Stuart's poetic development of his culturally bound sense of time. They are neither the poet Jesse Stuart nor flesh and blood Appalachians, but certain ones among them are archetypal embodiments of the Appalachian temporality concept. Through them, a whole culture is personified. Icie Hornbuckle does not tell the time on soft summer nights by looking at a luminescent wrist watch:

> Soft nights enchanted by this restless river
> Where fireflies tell the time instead of clocks.[3]

Neither does Fon Banks consult a calendar to discover where summer has gone:

> Where has the summer gone? Why is it ending
> From clouds of summer green to autumn brown?
> . . . .
> You know the green-cloud yesterdays have gone,
> Changed color and fled home down windy skies! (89)

In like manner, Wilson Smack does not need to check his birth certificate or the local courthouse records to know that his years have been fleeting:

> Corn stubbles stand as symbols of the years
> That have passed surely as the winds have
> blown. (163)

Mort Higgins must speak for his friend Don, a famed
hunter during his lifetime. Death, the greatest
hunter of them all, has run Don to ground:

> Time came along and took Don down the hill.
> He rests unmindful that the cottontail
> Plays on his lone brush-covered mound at will
> Beside the nest of eggs and setting quail. (94)

In direct contrast to these mountain personas
of Album and their observations of temporality is
Libbie Crownover, who rejects Appalachian temporality. Through her, one sees the temporality of
the dominant culture clashing directly with that
of the Appalachian subculture. Her time is not
their time and vice versa. Even though she loves
and wants to marry a young mountain man, she will
not. They are truly time-crossed lovers:

> Those deep dark hills are far too much to face
> Where people wear their lives away like weather,
> Where time and winds and weeds and rain efface
> The earth and crow caws measure wind-blue
> weather. (104)

As a result of his Appalachian sense of time,
Stuart deplores man's becoming a prisoner of the
clock and an extension of the machine, and his
fictional characters resent such dehumanization.
Theopolis Akers (The Good Spirit of Laurel Ridge)
measures time by what president was in office and
the nesting seasons of the birds. He tells his
city cousins he could not work at Dayton's Wright
Airfield where everyone rushes to and fro and fears
the atom bomb.[4]

Stuart recalls vividly the impact of the dominant culture's time concepts upon his life in The
Year of My Rebirth. It was nearly fatal. Working
in the Ashland steel mills as a young man saving
for college, Stuart had difficulty in keeping up

with a time that caused him to lose his stride in life and created eternal tension. At Lincoln Memorial and Vanderbilt, Jesse learned to make every minute count, and he had no time for butterflies and bees as a teacher and superintendent. In one year Stuart gave eighty-nine talks in thirty-nine states to help American schools in addition to publishing two books and a few short stories and articles. He had become the clock watcher, schedule maker and "speedy American" until his heart attack at Murray State College dropped him. To some extent it was his recovery of his native Appalachian sense of time that cured him. From January, 1955, until January, 1956, Stuart kept a journal and learned once again to listen to the earth's slow beating heart and recall childhood days when "time was flowing and eternal like an invisible river." One did not need a clock or watch to divide time into daytime, nighttime, and the four seasons. The day of week or hour of the day did not matter, and people were never hurried in "that constant tension of man-made time" that can grip a man in a vice.[5]

For Jesse Stuart and the Appalachian subculture, the human body was not patterned to be a dollars-and-cents machine and Stuart's characters wage a battle against the ruthless materialism of modern living. In Kentucky Is My Land the persona of "May I Lie Dead" would rather die than see his hills and Sandy River shaped to patterns.[6] In the short story "Bird Neck" a truly original character named Bird Neck foils the system by selling his body to the Goodland hospital for $25 then cheating them by hanging himself among the thick leaves of a tall tree where his skeleton is not discovered until winter bares the tree.[7]

In "Mad Davids and a Mechanical Goliath" Poodie Pitts and Shorty Prat do not have the same faith in time-saving machinery as does Hal Burton, operator of a big bulldozer, who tells these skeptical laborers his dozer cannot be stopped: "Damned thing might run over us! It looks like a big animal, but it doesn't have any sense." Poodie and Shorty cannot understand not being needed to use their long-handled shovels on the roadwork they have been doing for the State Highway Department for so many years.

55

They laugh and clank their shovels together in celebration when 10,000 little Davids (bees) stop the mighty Goliath (dozer).[8]

Appalachians thus refuse to march to the frenzied pace of the modern world, and they have come, by compulsion, to understand that technological unemployment is a threat to the human condition and exists only when a culture places more emphasis upon things rather than people:

> So people at Young's Fork were moved to non-legislative action. The shattered hulk of a $300,000 coal gouger lay 100 yards from the end of the scar. It had been dynamited a month before and totally wrecked. In its cab the sprung controls (Swing Left, Boom Down, Engine Throttle) no longer moved the boom's pendulous might and the red steel snout that had been rooting in the mountainside, capable of raising a 30,000-pound weight in one bite, lay slack-jawed."[9]

As an author Jesse Stuart has been occasionally accused of having a preoccupation with death, but his emphasis on the subject is purely Appalachian. The Appalachian does not make the same sharp divisions in time that the dominant culture does--past, present and future blend into a kind of perennial present, and many Appalachians can name their ancestors back to the American Revolution. Death does not end the presence of the deceased in the thinking, conversations and lives of Appalachians. Death is not amelioriated in the Appalachian sub-culture: its implications are endlessly discussed and thought about. Stuart's "preoccupation" with death is simply one inevitable reflection of Appalachian temporality. Many Stuart characters thus have an attitude toward death, and a rich system of accompanying symbols, that are incomprehensible to a member of the dominant culture.

Several of the older people among Stuart's fictional characters receive tokens (advance warnings) of their approaching deaths. As was the case with Melville's Queequeg, once the warning

comes they begin preparation for the ultimate
journey. In "Head of W-Hollow" Big Eif Porter
receives his token and prepares to die. He says
that a token can be many things: headless men,
forms of light, shepherd dogs and so forth.[10]
Anse Bushman receives his token (Trees of Heaven)
by being seriously injured while chopping a tree,
and he piously decides to throw away his pistol
and brass knuckles.[11] The irascible Grandpa Tussie
receives his token in the form of a spider snaring
a fly in the web above his sick bed, and in his
nightly deliriums he talks to his parents who have
come to take him "home."[12]

One universal time theme in the literature of
all cultures is the question of man's behavior when
he knows that time is running out. Foretaste of
Glory is a cosmically ironic analysis of that ultimate question as Stuart examines a gallery of characters who view the Northern Lights in Blakesburg
(Greenup, Kentucky) on September 18, 1941, and
assume that the Second Coming is at hand.

Some characters seize the occasion to settle
old differences before time is no more. Liam and
Booten Winston fight with knives in their mother's
boarding house.[13] Temp and Oll Spradling, husband
and wife, become intoxicated and fight publicly.

A whole series of characters settle affairs of
the heart. Pat Greenough and Aliss Dinwiddie, of
the town's two leading rival political families,
run over the riverbank to make love in the willows.
Judge Allie Anderson confesses to being the father
of the bastard Rufus Literal. The pious lawyer
Joe Oliver confesses to his wife that he's been
having an affair with the maid for fifteen years.
Ronnie Roundtree leaves his second wife and seven
children and returns to his first wife and two
children. And Mary Blanton, the town whore, is
terrified and prays fervently to "Sweet Jesus."

In all of the apocalyptic confusion, two voices
of reason fall upon unlistening ears. Ninety-year-
old Uncle Sweeter Dabney says he is not disturbed
because he believes that man cannot know the in-
finite. Reverend John Whetstone tells everyone

that the disturbance is the aurora borealis, but he is simply ignored and called a hypocrite. Both the philosopher and the minister are unheeded by Noah Billups, the town drunk, whose wife and children get dressed to go to heaven. Their youngest son cries because he can't take his little dog.

Despite the fact that Stuart is unsurpassed among American authors in embodying the temporality concept of his particular culture, he has been criticized throughout his career for the lack of "proper arrangement" in his works because of his "disturbing" use of the present tense. American critics have had no difficulty in accepting William Faulkner's tortured genealogy (i.e. Tomey's Terrel--Tennie's Jim in The Bear) or Thomas Wolfe's time-capsule journeys, because they are willing to believe that the brooding consciousness of Southern culture affects temporality in wonderfully strange ways.

Throughout his work, Jesse Stuart has commanded a time-obliterating lyricism as effectively as any other major American writer: he has accomplished this by using the perennial present of Appalachian temporality. Like the God of Joshua, Stuart can stop the sun in his literary heavens and suspend the normal order of things. In many of Stuart's works all of time becomes focused on a single point: the wind stops in the trees, sound is muffled and far away, the natural rhythms of earth are stopped, and the reader views the human soul escaped from time into a perennial present. In countless passages of Stuart, man is the leaf, the blossom and the bole dancing and swaying in the winds that blow before and after time.

Stuart's use of the perennial present make Jud Sparks and Didway Hargis, of Hie to the Hunters, as immortal as Tom Sawyer and Huckleberry Finn. In that brief summer and early autumn of boyhood before cultural stereotypes have hardened, Jud and Didway live the carefree and timeless days of youth in a mountain setting of hunting, trapping, dancing and following the whims of their fancy.

Another of Stuart's immortal youths who narrates from a perennial present is Sid Tussie of Taps for

<u>Private Tussie</u>. At that delicate stage between boyhood and manhood, Sid is constantly puzzled as to why adults have such short memories and behave in such strange and often contradictory ways. Unlike most adults, Sid does not believe time alters all things; he knows that beauty, truth and love are not negated by time. Sid cannot understand why his grandmother treats her daughter-in-law Vittie like an angel when Vittie has $10,000 and like a devil when Vittie's money runs out. He has the greatest difficulty in comprehending inconstancy in lovers. He observes his aunt Vittie, once so deeply in love with his uncle Kim, after Kim's death in World War II and her receiving $10,000. She is surrounded with new lovers and Sid is completely baffled. Stuart generates tremendous irony as Sid intermittently recalls the wind-torn and disintegrating American flags on the graves of mountain soldiers and observes Vittie's amorous cavortings with his uncles Mott and George.

In <u>Beyond Dark Hills</u> and <u>God's Oddling</u>, the narrator is seen as a youth, a young man and a mature adult defining himself in terms of his fathers and his home. His journey is the journey toward self-discovery and definition that all men undertake. In <u>Beyond Dark Hills</u> the youthful narrator refuses to step in his father's footsteps in the snow because he wants to make his own path in life. He goes on to travel beyond the dark confining hills of his birth to obtain a college education. He will return to the hills on his own terms. In <u>God's Oddling</u> the mature son returns to the same dark hills of his birth and recognizes them and his father, for the first time, in a tribute and discovery that only comes to few men who make the same journey through time. From the narrator of these two novels comes a powerful and sustained awareness of the timeless bond between all fathers and all sons. In a truly Appalachian conclusion, he realizes that not even his father's death can sever such a bond: "Knowing he is dead and buried, I still find it hard to believe he is gone. This is why I think I hear him when it is only the wind in the willow leaves. I think I hear his hoe turning the stones over again in his corn

row. How can he leave this world where his image
is stamped so indelibly upon everything? He is
still a part of this valley, just as it is still
a part of him."14

The impact that time invariably has upon
romantic love and young lovers is masterfully
portrayed in Trees of Heaven and Daughter of the
Legend. Their combined themes could be that even
if love does not ultimately suffice, it is the
only force in life that even comes close to con-
quering all. Tarvin Bushman and Subrinea Tussie
of Trees of Heaven and Dave Stoneking and Deutsia
Huntoon of Daughter of the Legend are archetypal
embodiments of the power of true love to alter
the normal dimensions of time--if only for a fleeting season. For these transformed pairs of young
lovers, the fact that the same transformation fails
to occur in the time-bound world about them is an
indictment of that other world, not of their own.

In Trees of Heaven Tarvin Bushman is the son
of Anse Bushman, a true mountain of man who long
since has forgotten about romantic love and for
whom time has become only money. He intimidates
all his neighbors in his unceasing efforts to amass
more land and money. Tarvin's love, Subrinea
Tussie, is the daughter of "squatters" who live on
uncleared land belonging to Anse, who hates her
family for not being exactly as he himself is.
The fact that Tarvin and Subrinea are beautiful in
their deep love for each other is of no importance
to their rival families. Stuart's description of
the young lovers' secret moonlight meetings, their
aching desire to consummate their love, and their
first night of love in the close heated quarters
of Tarvin's lambing shack--high on a winter mountain with baby lambs being born all about them--
touches the heart and touches eternity. Anse's
concern for the morrow looks paltry and mechanical
beside that vision.

In Daughter of the Legend Dave Stoneking and
the beautiful Melungeon, Deutsia Huntoon, must fight
the time-bound prejudices of "race" and social
class. Dave, a young man from a middle class
Virginia family, ultimately threatens his best

60

friend with an ax for speaking against the woman of his choice. Dave, fair and blond, and Deutsia, dark with golden blond hair, enjoy too brief a season of love. Through Stuart's masterful employment of foreshadowing, one has a gnawing and building suspicion that for them time is running out and love will not conquer all.

On one of their first dates, they take a long walk by Clinch River. They stop at a country store near a "blue hole" in the river, a place known for an undercurrent which can pull under even the strongest of swimmers. The old folks at the store see that they only have eyes for each other, and the old ones smile and tell them a life of working in corn and tobacco, childbearing and Time will bend them and frost their hair. On another night Dave and Deutsia spend a night in the shelter of a rock cliff to avoid the severity of a storm lashing outside their rock "home." Time runs out for them during a wildly stormy night the following spring as Deutsia hemorrhages to death during the birth of Dave Huntoon Stoneking. Without Deutsia, Dave cannot bear to remain on Sanctuary Mountain. However, he leaves the newborn son to be reared by his "Melungeon" grandparents—mainly because he wants the son to grow up with the temporality concept of hill people.

Throughout Stuart's works the passage of time is irrevocable and, as was the case with Thomas Wolfe, one cannot go home again. In Stuart's portrayal of Appalachia, a few characters do attempt to relive "the old party of the long ago," but all are met with devastating disappointment. Typical is Burt Hoskins, who conducts a middle-aged odyssey in the short story "Lost Land of Youth."

Like many men Burt has an overwhelming desire to recapture the beauty and vitality of his youth and the period of first love. As a successful middle-aged man living outside his native Appalachian culture, he returns on an autumnal journey through sun drenched years to attend a Lost Creek funeral and search for his young love Mollie Didway. He cannot recognize her face among the crowd.[15] Through Stuart's masterful handling of the story's

61

time motif of autumnal tones, the reader is left
with a flushed face, a dry mouth and a dull ache
in the throat. It is ourselves--not Burt--we weep
for.

Those who have criticized Stuart for his "disturbing" use of the present tense do Stuart, his
Appalachian characters, and themselves a great disservice. C. G. Jung's observations regarding the
time concept of Pueblo Indians and the dominant
culture's failure to understand or permit that time
concept are equally applicable to Stuart's literary
world of Appalachians and its critical reception:

We are solely in need of a Truth or
a self-understanding similar to that of
Ancient Egypt, which I have found still
living with the Taos Pueblos. Their chief
of ceremonies, old Ochwiay (Mountain Lake),
said to me: "We are the people who live
on the roof of the world, we are the sons
of the Sun, who is our father. We help
him daily to rise and to cross over the
sky. We do this not only for ourselves,
but for the Americans also. Therefore
they should not interfere with our religion. But if they continue to do so
(by missionaries) and hinder us, then
they will see that in ten years the sun
will rise no more."
He correctly assumes that their day,
their light, their consciousness and
their meaning will die, when destroyed
through the narrowmindedness of American
Rationalism, and the same will happen
to the whole world, when subjected to
such treatment.[16]

Jack Weller, mentioned earlier as a member of
the dominant culture who shared the life of Appalachians over a period of years, came to an appreciation of the Appalachian time sense as an ironic
blessing which has prepared Appalachians to live
successfully in the automated world of the future:

The cybernetic age is coming rapidly--
the age when we must redefine the worth

62

of man in terms other than the nature
of his work and the size of his income.
Making such a redefinition will not be
easy, for it will require a complete
change in our concepts and our philosophy of life, as well as in our activities.
When our life situation becomes transformed by the cybernetic revolution, it
may well be that the mountaineer will already have the concept of life and work
fit for the new age."[17]

Throughout the works of Jesse Stuart, time
is masterfully and imaginatively handled, just as
it is in the works of William Faulkner or Thomas
Wolfe. Jesse Stuart's characters simply march to
the time of an Appalachian drummer.

NOTES

1. Marion Pearsall, <u>Little Smoky Ridge: The Natural History of a Southern Appalachian Neighborhood</u> (University: University of Alabama Press, 1959), pp. 81-87.

2. Jesse Stuart, <u>Man With a Bull-Tongue Plow</u> (New York: E. P. Dutton, 1934), p. 150.

3. Jesse Stuart, <u>Album of Destiny</u> (New York: E. P. Dutton, 1944), p. 237.

4. Jesse Stuart, <u>The Good Spirit of Laurel Ridge</u> (New York: McGraw-Hill, 1953), p. 155.

5. Jesse Stuart, <u>The Year of My Rebirth</u> (New York: McGraw-Hill, 1956), pp. 4-8, 124-125.

6. Jesse Stuart, <u>Kentucky Is My Land</u> (New York: E. P. Dutton, 1952), p. 56.

7. Jesse Stuart, <u>Plowshare in Heaven</u> (New York: McGraw-Hill, 1956), pp. 179-184.

8. Jesse Stuart, <u>Come Gentle Spring</u> (New York: McGraw-Hill, 1969), pp. 121, 122, 129.

9. Paul Good, "Kentucky's Coal Beds of Sedition," in <u>Appalachia in the Sixties</u>, ed. by David S. Walls and John B. Stephenson (Lexington, Ky.: University Press of Kentucky, 1972), pp. 188-189.

10. Jesse Stuart, <u>Head O' W-Hollow</u> (New York: E. P. Dutton, 1936), p. 19.

11. Jesse Stuart, <u>Trees of Heaven</u> (New York: E. P. Dutton, 1940), p. 334.

12. Jesse Stuart, <u>Taps for Private Tussie</u> (New York: The World Publishing Company, 1969), p. 277.

13. Jesse Stuart, <u>Foretaste of Glory</u> (New York: E. P. Dutton, 1946), p. 14.

14. Jesse Stuart, God's Oddling (New York: McGraw-Hill, 1960), p. 266.

15. Jesse Stuart, Come Back to the Farm (New York: McGraw-Hill, 1971), pp. 198-201.

16. Miguel Serrano, C. G. Jung and Hermann Hesse, trans. Frank MacShane (New York: Shocken Books, 1972), pp. 87-88.

17. Jack E. Weller, Yesterday's People (Lexington, Ky.: University of Kentucky Press, 1965), pp. 159-160.

JESSE
STUART
COUNTRY

CHAPTER FOUR

TERRITORIALITY

Appalachians maintain a vital man-nature
identity that held good for all Americans only
during the frontier period. In the Appalachian
subculture, land is not something to use like
gasoline or toothpaste and no man can really ever
own it because it is eternal. The only valid title
to land is love: a man can own land in his heart
as much or more than the man who has a legal deed
to it.

As Thomas Wolfe truly said regarding the
Appalachians' land mystique, the mountains are
their masters, and go home to their eyes before
they reach the age of five, and whatever they say
or do must forever remain hillbound.[1] One of
Jesse Stuart's poetic creations, Dossie McKee,
best expresses this deep feeling for land:

As oaks that root deep in Kentucky earth
And these eternal juts of rock that stand,
I stand with these dark hills that gave me
birth
With plow and hoe and slopes of sedge grass
land.
. . . .
These hills are closer to me than my skin,
My roof could be the sky, my bed the rocks;
My only music the night blowing wind,
The pouring rivers and the barking fox.

The poetry, novels, and short stories of Jesse
Stuart derive a great deal of their power from the
author's ability to use the earth as a great mother
from which his art is born and sustained: "People
of the Appalachians look upon their land—even if
it fails to produce as well as land in other sec-
tions of the country—as a living thing. They have
seen its creativity in plants that they cultivated
tenderly with hoe and horse plow. Thus, their land
and their plants are dearer to them than if they

67

had been cultivated by machinery."[3]

The whole of nature is fused in the works of Stuart and man is truly one with the elements. Stuart is without superior in American literature not only as a naturalist but in his skill in using nature as a theme running throughout his literary production. On this basis his work ranks squarely with Thoreau's Walden, Cape Cod, and A Week on the Concord and Merrimack Rivers.

In 1944, after painstaking revision, Stuart published what he has long considered his mountain poetic urn, Album of Destiny.[4] As is true of Man With A Bull-Tongue Plow, Album of Destiny is one of the great works of American poetry in its artistic metamorphoses of man. The seasons of nature are the seasons of man who is leaf, flower, earth, wind and sky. Man is a product of the earth: a toiler upon the earth who returns to the earth. He is plant, bird and fox.

The closeness of man to the four seasons, the bond between man and earth, and the poet's ultimate recognition of the oneness of man and earth are three vital themes that help give Album its greatness. The four distinct seasons of the Appalachian mountains are employed by Stuart and give a oneness to the poetic world. Spring is the time of planting, summer is the season of work, autumn is the time of harvest and winter is the time of desolation when one must be sustained by the fruits of his toil.

The personas of Album of Destiny--John and Kathleen Sutton, their twelve children, and various of their neighbors--could well be the Appalachian ethos speaking through generations in regard to youth, death, love, hate, work, and the four seasons of man and nature. Copperhead, blacksnake, lizard, scorpion and wind are additional personas commenting on the nature of existence and presenting moral alternatives to this varied gallery of human perspectives.

The reader is introduced to John and Kathleen Sutton in the spring of the earth and of their love

68

in collections of poems entitled "Prologue,"
"Whispering Grass" and "Sonatas of Spring."
John and Kathleen are in love in the April of
their life in a world of "wind-organs in green
seas of leaves" (26), of "green-dark nights" (27)
and of "sweet wine-colored wind," a world where
spring is the promise of new life:

> Give man green velvet earth and light green
> wind;
> Give man the world where he can own his heart,
> And own his brains and breathe no smoke-dyed
> wind;
> New earth where he can play the different
> part. (25)

Subsequently, "Songs of the Summer Sun" present John and Kathleen and their neighbors in their
summer of life working for their families. The
speaker of "Kathleen" captures the industry and
the ripeness of these poems depicting the summer
of life:

> I love the harvest moon, the drifting skies;
> I love the wild rose petals on the hills
> And July wheat stacks filled with wild bird
> cries,
> Life-ever-lasting, drying, snail-thin shells.
> I love oak bark, the lizard's tight-lipped
> mouth;
> The red sweet Williams growing on a bank;
> The little streams of swallows going south,
> And horseweeds by the river growing rank.
> I love blue glimmer of cornfield haze,
> And such slow passing of the summer days. (77)

John and Kathleen's summer songs are inevitably
replaced by "Songs of Approaching Autumn." Kathleen
realizes their lives are turning in a new and final
direction:

> Come closer to me, John, why are we here?
> The flowers are dead, the butterflies have
> fled;
> They have gone somewhere with the faded year,
> Where leaves have gone, the drifting
> crimson-red

That flow out of the woods' wind-streams
(of blood)
And spatter on the wind beneath the sky. (119)

John and Kathleen have had their spring of love
and their summer of twelve children. Now their
love sustains them against the approaching winter:

Not even autumn, with his sad refrain
Of old sweet music from the dying leaf,
Can make their love for one another vain;
They've loved too long and known the
cutting grief
That sometimes marrows into brain and
heart. (121)

Finally, the poems of "Songs of The Silent
Snow" provide a mountain requiem for John and
Kathleen, who are sleeping under the winter snow.
They will be unable to heed the spring dawn's call
to new life and work. John would not have men die
who love life so much (167).

Throughout Album of Destiny the lesser creatures of the earth also experience the seasons of
life and, like man, they ponder the meaning of
their lives and destinies. Viewed from Stuart's
perspective of the universe, however, neither their
world nor their ponderings are smaller than man's:

Gray lizard looks down on the yellow light
Of stars and moon; Gray lizard wonders why
He lies behind the bark of blackoak tree
Under the pretty blue of the night sky,
Wondering about his lizard-destiny.
Blow over him you wind, and smile, you moon,
And, stars, laugh from your blue oblivion.(215)

Album of Destiny is thus a luxuriant mountain tap-
estry with man occupying the center space. Above
him are the oak trees of the mountain and the stars;
below him are the singing streams and the lesser
creatures of the earth. One of the book's poetic
spokesmen, Robert Diesel, thanks God he can see the
beauty of autumn because he is one with "this garnered soil, this fruited tree" (141). In view of
the book's matchless embodiment of the Appalachian

70

ethos, _Album of Destiny_ is one of the most abundantly fruited trees in the garnered soil of
American poetry.

Hold _April_ develops the same timeless ties
between Appalachians and their land as _Man With A
Bull-Tongue Plow_ and _Album of Destiny_. It is a
highly polished book which shows Jesse Stuart as
one of America's finest poets. Portions of two
poems--"The snow lies patched" and "Hold April"--
are sufficient to indicate the book's quality and
the continuing role of the land as the great mother
of Stuart's poetic art:

> The snow lies patched on our enduring hills
> Where surfaces first face the morning sun;
> Snow-water mumbles down slow winter rills
> But stops when sunset freezing has begun.
> And winter birds seek shelter for the night
> In fodder shocks and in the frozen grass
> And shadows of owls' wings in pale moonlight
> Frighten the timid rabbits when they pass.
> And then to see an evening silhouette
> Of snow-patched crazy quilt against the moon,
> Enduring beauty one cannot forget
> That cannot come too often or too soon.[5]
> . . . .

> Hold on to April; never let her pass!
> Another year before she comes again
> To bring us wind as clean as polished glass
> And apple blossoms in soft, silver rain.
> Hold April when there's music in the air,
> When life is resurrected like a dream,
> When wild birds sing up flights of windy stair
> And bees love alder blossoms by the stream.
> . . . . (87)

The fictional and autobiographical novels and
short stories of Jesse Stuart are as firmly tied
to the land as are his thousands of poems. As a
young graduate student leaving Vanderbilt university, Stuart was advised by the famous literary
critic Donald Davidson: "Go back to your country.
. . . Go back and write of your country as the
Irish have written of Ireland."[6] From the 1930's
until the present, Stuart has heeded this advice

and anchored his poetry and prose to the land and the people he knows better than any other author ever has. In Stuart's prose, as in his poetry, he cites the land as the source from which the total work grows and takes form: "Too many youth and too many teachers think to be a writer, one must first find the big dream. But I believe, he must first find the small white hair-roots that will go down and give growth to the plant. The writer is the plant. Creativity is the dream. So it is from the tiny little seed the plant will expand and grow into the big dream."[7]

In a review of one of Stuart's earliest collections of short stories--Men of the Mountains, Lewis Gannett, writing in the New York Herald Tribune, recognized and appreciated this organic inevitability which flows throughout Stuart's work; Gannett appreciated the great artistry that underlies the easy naturalness of Stuart's style and knew that not just anyone could stumble into the Appalachian mountains and emerge with such literary art: "No man could go into the hills and write this stuff; he must have lived there. . . . there is a singing strength to Jesse Stuart's mountain prose, and his familiar story seems no more banal than the coming of another spring. He is not writing about quaint hillfolk, you feel, and this is his unique quality: through him the back hollows speak in their own tongue."[8]

Jesse Stuart's home in W-Hollow near Greenup, Kentucky, has been both a working and a literary farm. In addition to producing hay, tobacco, cattle, corn, garden vegetables and fruit, it has produced many of Stuart's unforgettable characters. Stuart has maintained that he has wanted all the people who have lived on his acres as tenants to be characters: "I want people who live on my land to be characters and many of them have been. They have been colorful characters--characters that appeal to world readers. They are a microcosm of world humanity."[9] The prototypes of the Tussies, Op Akers and Mick Powderjay (Jesse's father in God's Oddling) are but a few of the Stuart characters who have dwelt on his acres. All of them have great respect and deep feeling for the land.

72

Among Jesse Stuart's tall figures of earth, to lose one's ties with the land is to lose the quality of life, if not life itself. In Trees of Heaven Subrinea Tussie's family have become tenants on their own property by selling their timber rights to a lumber company. They cannot pay their property taxes and thus lose their shack, land and family burial ground to their prosperous land-wolfing neighbor, Anse Bushman, to whom land has become only money. Both Subrinea and her family of "worthless" Tussies fight desperately against Anse's attempt to cut and sell the only virgin timber left on the property--the towering trees of heaven--the aged and beautiful alianthus trees, which send down their massive roots to hold and protect the hillside graves of generations of the Tussie dead.

Through Grandpa Tussie, the beloved rascal and family patriarch of the Welfare Tussies, Jesse Stuart provides a vital insight into the meaning of land ownership and the lack of that ownership within the Appalachian subculture. Near the end of his life Grandpa buys the first farm he has ever owned with part of the insurance money received from his son's war "death": a fifty-acre piece of scraggly mountain hillside. Pathetically, Grandpa realizes too late the abiding value of independent ownership of land. His realization that he will not be there the following spring to teach his grandson Sid the basics of making a hillside-farm living is truly tragic:

> Grandpa never cared whether he had anything or not and when he did have something everbody was welcome to it. I'd never seen another man like Grandpa. The only thing he'd ever had he didn't want to part with was his land.
> . . . .
> "When you raise your own corn, beans, taters, and pumpkins, you don't haf to wonder and worry about how long you are a-goin to hold your relief and about somebody a-reportin you. And you can vote the way you please. It's better than dependin on the old-age pension

checks of nine dollars a month after
you get sixty-five, fer ye and yer old
woman--if you vote as you please. You
don't get but seven dollars if you
don't vote right. Farmin is the only
sure way."

"Don't talk about farmin now, Press,"
Grandma opened the door and said. "I've
been a-listenin and it hurts me to hear
you talk. We ought to've done it long
ago."

"But I didn't have land of my own,"
Grandpa said. "I didn't have dirt black
as a crow's wing."[10]

Perhaps the greatest dramatic embodiment of
the ways the Appalachian's relationship to the land
differs from that of the modern suburban American
is found in Op Akers of The Good Spirit of Laurel
Ridge, and the differences are many. The prototype
of Op was George Alexander: a man who lived on
Stuart's farm for many years, a man who never went
to doctors, a man who could outwork men half his
age and a man whom Stuart refers to as "a local
Henry David Thoreau."[11]

In The Good Spirit of Laurel Ridge Op Akers
lives on Laurel Ridge of the Little Sandy country,
and he is one with himself and the whole earth.
The rhythms and patterns of his beautifully simple
existence provide an early antidote in modern American literature to the nerve pollution brought on
by the hectic life style of the atomic age.

Op observes his nephew and his nephew's wife,
who have come from Dayton, Ohio, to share his
simple home and life for a summer. As is generally
the case with rural Americans, confronted with
urban ones, he notices the tenseness and high-strung
nature of his guests during the first days following
their arrival, and he is glad when they finally can
relax enough to calm down.

Op is self-sufficient. He cultivates a small
garden, harvests edible wild greens, hunts, fishes,
and sells nuts and berries in the small town of
Honeywell. Like countless Appalachians, he has an

expert naturalist's awareness of the flora and
fauna of the mountains, and he doctors himself
with "yarbs" (herb remedies) (45).

Op's Laurel Ridge country of sprangling
streams is his Walden and like Thoreau he drinks
at the stream of life but sees its sandy bottom.
As was equally true of Thoreau, Op is not afraid
to lie down and take a nap because of the paranoid
fear that something might happen in the world while
he slumbers. Op's favorite entertainment is in
listening to the wind blowing through his homemade
horse hair wind harp, and he simply refuses to share
the nervous ticking of modern existence. Op does
not advocate his way of life; he lives it.

During his lifetime, Jesse Stuart has bought
and combined a series of small farms that his parents had rented from various landlords when Stuart
was a boy, and his family's experiences on this
land have provided the basis for many of his fictional biographical novels. God's Oddling, an
autobiographical novel depicting the close ties of
the Stuart family to each other and to the abiding
land,is typical of Stuart's ability to achieve universality through particularity. Only after leaving the mountains, becoming highly educated and
traveling through the world, does the author return
home and know both it and his "earth-educated"
father--perhaps for the first time.

From the pages of God's Oddling, Jesse Stuart's
parents emerge as people of little formal education.
Martha Hilton Stuart finished the second grade and
could read and write with difficulty. Mitchell
Stuart had no formal education and could barely
sign his name. But in God's Oddling both parents
emerge as people who have a wisdom and beauty that
is old as the earth and a type of innate dignity
that no man can acquire from just reading books or
traveling. Mitch Stuart, in particular, emerges
as a man who traveled much in W-Hollow:

> Many people thought my father was just
> a one-horse farmer who never got much out
> of life. They saw only a little man dressed
> in clean, patched overalls with callused and

brier-scratched hands. They often saw
the beard along his face. And they saw
him go off and just stand in a field
and look at something. They thought he
was moody. Well, he was that all right,
but when he was standing there and people thought he was looking into space,
he was looking at a flower or mushroom
or a new bug he'd discovered for the
first time. And when he looked up into
a tree, he wasn't searching for a hornet's
nest to burn or a bird's nest to rob.
He wasn't trying to find a bee tree.
He was just looking closely at the beauty
in a tree. And among the millions, he
always found one different enough to
excite him.
      No one who really knew him ever felt
sorry for my father. Any feeling of pity
turned to envy. For my father had a world
of his own, larger and richer than the
vast earth that world travelers know.
He found more beauty in his acres and
square miles than poets who have written
a half-dozen books. Only my father
couldn't write down the words to express
his thoughts. He had no common symbols
by which to share his wealth. He was a
poet who lived his life upon this earth
and never left a line of poetry--except
to those of us who lived with him.[12]

In many of Jesse Stuart's short stories, the
Stuart land emerges as a teacher of man regarding
the basic principles of life--Frost's "old truths
we keep coming back to." In "The Builders and the
Dream" the Stuart family must all work hard to build
their home and raise corn and tobacco.[13] The fifty-
year-old mother of "A Mother's Place is With Her
Son" works from before dawn until dusk with her
sons in the cornfield. She is teaching her youngest
son, who has been sent home from college for hell
raising, the abiding value of hard labor, sweat
and honesty.[14] "Victory and The Dream" is the
story of sixteen-year-old Shan Powderjay's plowing,
cultivating, and planting an eight-acre field in
one week of high school spring vacation; accom-

76

plishing this awesome task makes the young man feel that he will never be defeated again and that his dreams of graduating from college can be realized by his own efforts.[15]

In The Year of My Rebirth, the land is the healer of those who will listen to the words she whispers but never shouts. The recuperating artist notices once again the dark beauty of January mountains; winter white oaks in the wind; "something soft and whispering and songlike" in a winter thaw; "beautiful wet, cloud rising" February days; the pewees' March return; the early greening of Hazelnut bushes and weeping willows; and the earth's slow beating April heart.[16]

In addition to anchoring his poetry, short stories, and novels firmly to the Appalachian earth, Stuart has published numerous expository prose articles as one of America's finest lay authorities on Appalachian flora and fauna. His series of articles "Under My Sky," published during the mid-1950's by the Louisville Courier Journal, is vintage Thoreau in quality. Stuart has published similar articles dealing with the whole question of ecology in publications ranging from The American Forests to The Progressive Farmer. This facet of his work would make up a book that is yet to be compiled.

Though Stuart's employment of the land and its people has often been misunderstood by those who have no knowledge of the Appalachian subculture, those who describe his work as "picturesque" do both themselves and the author a great disservice: "He writes about side-hill farmers, moonshiners and loggers, not because they are picturesque but because they are his own people. More often he writes about the land itself . . . because it is his own land, because he knows the smell of it when his plow turns it over and the feel of it between his toes."[17]

Like his fictional Deutsia Huntoon of Daughter of the Legend, who knows the location and nature of every little stream, and every flower, tree, vine and briar of Sanctuary Mountain, Stuart has

maintained an intensely deep, mystical, often
misunderstood rapport with the dark hills of his
literary creations: "No one will believe it when
I tell him the voice of my land and the whole universe is in constant communication with me. Mes-
sages come in so loud, so strong and clear and in
sound which only I understand, that I find myself
talking back. I am in oneness with the land and
everything thereon. The winds and streams make
symphonies for me. And no one will believe me
when I say I am brother to the tree."[18]

Stuart is fully aware of the great debt he
owes to the land for the nourishment it has provided him both as a farmer and as an artist: "As
I grow older, I constantly rediscover the beauty
of the land where I was born and where I still live
today. This valley becomes more valuable and precious to me every day. It has been and still is
the source of my work as a writer. One day as I
walked over my land, I remembered that I wasn't
the only writer who had explored and used his own
backyard for inspiration. Emily Dickinson, Henry
David Thoreau, Nathaniel Hawthorne, and Robert
Frost are just four who have done so. And so I
was grateful to the land for what it had given me
as a human being and as a writer."[19]

In the literary world of Stuart there is no
clear-cut line of separation between man and earth,
nor is there the expectation that the natural world
should be any more or less idyllic than it actually
is. The whole of animate and inanimate nature
blends in Stuart's work. The W-Hollow road in
dusty autumn is the color of a pied copperhead;
winter white oaks groan restlessly in the wind,
like old people rising up and their bones popping;[21]
mountain clouds are groundhogs "bilin" (boiling)
their coffee;[22] and Gabriel will sound an old fox
horn on judgment day to summon the Plum Grove dead.[23]

C. G. Jung's reaction to the Pueblo Indians'
oneness with the land could be equally applied to
Jesse Stuart's Appalachians: "Thank God, there is
still a man who has not learned how to think, but
still perceives his thoughts as though they were
visions or living beings, and who perceives his

gods as though they were visible thoughts, based
on instinctive reality. He has made peace with
his gods, and they live with him. It is true that
the life he leads is close to nature. It is full
of hope, of brutality, misery, sickness and death;
nevertheless, it has a completeness, a satisfaction
and an emotional beauty which is unfathomable."[24]

On December 7, 1979, Jesse Stuart and his
wife Naomi Deane donated half of their beloved
1,000-acre W-Hollow farm (assessed value $1.47
million) to the state of Kentucky to be used as
a nature preserve. The other half was purchased
from the Stuarts with state and federal money.
During the dedication ceremonies of the Jesse
Stuart Nature Preserve, Kentucky Governor Julian
Carroll acknowledged the literary value of the
farm as well as its value as a nature preserve.
One of the first hiking trails to be opened on
the preserve is in the Shinglemill Hollow, where
Stuart wrote "Shinglemill Symphony" as well as
"Love Song for Over 40." The Stuarts have kept
a small plot of land surrounding their home and
continue to live there.[25]

NOTES

1. Thomas Wolfe, Look Homeward Angel (New York: Charles Scribner's Sons, 1957), p. 352.

2. Jesse Stuart, Album of Destiny (New York: E. P. Dutton, 1944), p. 107.

3. Jesse Stuart, "Ascend the High Mountain," Country Beautiful, Feb. 1962, 13.

4. Everetta Love Blair, Jesse Stuart; His Life and Works (Columbia, S. C.: University of South Carolina Press, 1967), pp. 41-42.

5. Jesse Stuart, Hold April (New York: McGraw-Hill, 1962), pp. 54-55.

6. Jesse Stuart, "I Have to Write or Die," Christian Action, Dec. 1959, p. 19.

7. Jesse Stuart, "Straths in the Green Valley Below," American Forests, Aug. 1968, 12.

8. Lewis Gannett, "Men of the Mountains," review of Men of the Mountains, by Jesse Stuart, in News of Books and Authors, January-May 1941, p. 22.

9. Jesse Stuart, "Characters Versus Farmers," Phi Kappa Phi Journal, LII (Winter 1972), 26.

10. Jesse Stuart, Taps for Private Tussie (New York: The World Publishing Company, 1969), pp. 263, 271.

11. Stuart, "Characters Versus Farmers," p. 27.

12. Jesse Stuart, "Oddling in Patched Pants," Glenmary's Challenge, Autumn 1969, 15.

13. Jesse Stuart, Come Back to the Farm (New York: McGraw-Hill, 1971), pp. 105-116.

14. Jesse Stuart, My Land Has A Voice (New York: McGraw-Hill, 1966), pp. 98-106.

15. Stuart, <u>Come</u> <u>Back</u> <u>to</u> <u>the</u> <u>Farm</u>, pp. 55-76.

16. Jesse Stuart, <u>The</u> <u>Year</u> <u>of</u> <u>My</u> <u>Rebirth</u> (New York: McGraw-Hill, 1956), p. 36.

17. Malcolm Cowley, "Man With a Bull-Tongue Plow," review of <u>Man</u> <u>With</u> <u>a</u> <u>Bull-Tongue</u> <u>Plow</u>, by Jesse Stuart, in <u>New</u> <u>Republic</u>, Oct. 31, 1934, p. 342.

18. Stuart, "Straths in the Green Valley Below," p. 53.

19. Jesse Stuart, <u>A</u> <u>Jesse</u> <u>Stuart</u> <u>Reader</u> (New York: McGraw-Hill, 1963), p. 178.

20. Jesse Stuart, <u>Head</u> <u>O'</u> <u>W-Hollow</u> (New York: E. P. Dutton, 1936), p. 3.

21. Stuart, <u>The</u> <u>Year</u> <u>of</u> <u>My</u> Rebirth, p. 35.

22. Stuart, <u>The</u> <u>Good</u> <u>Spirit</u> <u>of</u> <u>Laurel</u> <u>Ridge</u>, p. 154.

23. Jesse Stuart, <u>Tales</u> <u>From</u> <u>the</u> <u>Plum</u> <u>Grove</u> <u>Hills</u> (New York: E. P. Dutton, 1946), p. 250.

24. Miguel Serrano, <u>C.</u> <u>G.</u> <u>Jung</u> <u>and</u> <u>Hermann</u> <u>Hesse</u>, trans. by Frank MacShane (New York: Shocken Books, 1972), p. 53.

25. "A natural gift; Jesse Stuart turns over part of farm for preserve," Louisville (Ky.) <u>Courier</u> <u>Journal</u>, 9 Dec. 1979, Sec. B, p. 1.

Jesse and Naomi, October 15, 1954

CHAPTER FIVE

BISEXUALITY

As depicted by Jesse Stuart, the Appalachian
subculture is marked by an extreme bisexuality,
a trait that makes itself felt most notably in the
importance the culture attaches to violence and
love. The Appalachian family is patriarchal, and
masculinity symbols reinforce the concept of the
male as a creature to be respected or even feared.
The mountain man asks no one's permission to do
anything; his aggressive individualism is tempered
only by his deep love for his dependents and connections. This definition of the male as "no one
to mess with" led to the notorious period of Appalachian feuds, "one of the most fantastic dramas
in American history. . . . in savagery and stark
horror they dwarf the cattle wars of the Great
Plains and, by contrast, make the vendettas of
Sicily look like children's parlor games."[1] But
the personalisation that such bisexuality brings
with it has also created an extremely rich family
life based on loyalty, love, and mutual respect.
Stuart's work mirrors both of these developments
with its customary accuracy.

Jesse Stuart is no stranger to violence: It
has occurred throughout his lifetime and art, and
while as an artist he has never glorified violence
for its own sake, he has successfully employed it
as one major and vital theme in his poetry, novels,
and short stories.

An article in *Time* magazine of November 7,
1938, recounted perhaps the most famous violent
incident in the life of the "Greenup Poet" and
expressed the fear that "the pugnacious Stuart
inheritance" might "wreck the career of one of
the most promising U.S. poets." Because of his
expressing an opposing political philosophy, Stuart
had been physically attacked by a local constable.
Time's description of the Stuart clan and their

friends during the subsequent courtroom scene is indicative of the older and traditional masculine ethic of Appalachians. Most of the spectators came armed. One spectator observed, "There would have been a little excitement if a firecracker had gone off." During this time of trouble Jesse was offered the full support of his uncle Marion Stuart: "Last week 86-year-old Uncle Marion Stuart, who lives at Twelve Pole, W. Va., heard of Jesse's troubles. Uncle Marion, celebrated by Jesse because he killed his last man at 81, dug a well at 83, and built a house to retire in at 85, wrote to Jesse: 'Have they caught the fellow who jumped you? If they haven't, I'll be along presently and help you bring him to justice.'"[2]

Early in his career, Jesse Stuart announced his intention to portray the violent world of his Appalachia: "In 1937 I was given a Guggenheim Fellowship and visited twenty-seven countries in Europe. After fourteen months I came back to the farm and started a little newspaper. I wrote my first editorials on a Congressman, was trailed and beaten up. I have been shot at twice, cut once with a knife, yet I'm very much alive, and if I continue to be alive--so help me God--I'll portray the section of America that gave me birth."[3] Stuart has never wavered in portraying the Appalachian subculture in its totality, particularly in his embodiment of the bisexually orientated individualism of the Appalachian people.

A multitude of personas in Man With a Bull-Tongue Plow and Album of Destiny reveal various aspects of the marked bisexuality of the Appalachian subculture. Mart Shelton, the father of five sons and three daughters, works hard and lays down his ideas like stones in a well-built wall. He makes his sons "step" and he supervises his daughters' behavior very closely. He has raised his family well and he doesn't care a 'tinker's damn' about what other people think of his philosophy; he is a man "not afraid of Hell."[4] The intoxicated persona of sonnets 163 and 164 will not join his beloved Jean Elizabeth in church: He does not want her to see him stagger while walking down the aisle. He is "as high as a Kentucky pine" and in no mood to hear a sermon on the evils of whiskey, women, cards and sweet wine.

In "Rhett Speaks of Sebie" Rhett bemoans the fact that modern hill sons are a softer race who have turned to books and are afraid to blister their hands in toil on the rugged hillside land.[5] Mart Tussie speaks in behalf of his dead friend Cy Hailey and tells the grass that it does not have the right to tattle tale to the wind about how much Cy loved whiskey, women, guns and working shirtless in the sun (190). Trueman Abdon praises his hill wife Joan for having the right priorities:

> Joan is a hill wife for a mountain man
> And solid as these hills that hold her here,
> As loyal to her husband as her clan . . . (83)

The rigid bisexuality of the Appalachian family system is reflected in various Stuart novels. In God's Oddling, Stuart's tribute to his father Mick, Mick left his wife and family for one whole summer and returned to "his people" on the Big Sandy because his patriarchal authority was questioned in his own household: his wife had refused to let him throw her drunken brother, the legendary Uncle Jeff, out of their home. In this novel, Mick is a drinking man but in typical Appalachian fashion he respects his wife's prerogative and will not bring moonshine whiskey into the house. Rather, he stashes it in the loft of the log barn where, late and early, he ascends to partake of the healing fount. Even in Taps for Private Tussie, Stuart's satire of the mountain welfare system, Press Tussie is the undisputed leader of his own immediate family and the hordes of "welfare Tussies."

This intense emphasis upon maleness by the Appalachian subculture is one vital factor contributing to Appalachians' intense pride in family history and willingness to defend family honor. It is significant that such an early work as Beyond Dark Hills begins with a detailed account of Stuart's ancestors. This pride in ancestry has inevitably led to close family unity within the Appalachian family system, and family pride often extends beyond the grave. Stuart describes his Grandfather Mitchell

Stuart, who fought a lifelong battle with the
Houndshell family, as a man whom one might consider
a perfect example of the traditional Appalachian
patriarch: "Grandpa said he never wanted to be
buried near a Houndshell when he died. He said if
a Houndshell went to Hell he didn't want to go.
Said he'd had enough of the Houndshells here on
earth. If they meet in the same place there will
be war in either Heaven or Hell, I fear."[6] Several
years after Grandpa Mitch had 'gone to his reward,'
Jesse, while working in the Ashland steel mills in
Boyd County, Kentucky, was forced into fighting a
man over Grandpa Mitch's reputation in neighboring
Lawrence County.

Many Appalachian men and many Stuart characters
have the reputation of being dangerous. Uncle Kim
of Taps For Private Tussie is a typical example.
He is such a noted expert with pistol, rifle, and
shotgun that he is feared by everyone--including
the sheriff and the deputies, even though Kim is
not a bad man. When the sheriff and his deputies
come to the Tussie home periodically to arrest Kim
for minor offenses, they can never catch him un-
aware, and he runs out the back door and hides on
the mountain, from which he playfully takes near-
missing shots at the law officers. In modern Appalachia there are still men like Kim--men whom all
legal officials allow a wide margin, an understood
mountain detente.

In Stuart's education-autobiographical novels,
the educator is often forced to physically fight
for the educational process to be allowed to continue in mountain classrooms. The young narrator
of The Thread That Runs So True must fight Guy
Hawkins, a pupil older and larger than he, who had
previously whipped the narrator's sister--the former
teacher of Lonesome Valley School. Guy returns
after school and tells his teacher that one of them
will have to go and Guy does--in the first round.
Following this cathartic session with his "guidance
counsellor," Guy becomes a model pupil and after
news of the teacher's victory spreads throughout
the hollows, Lonesome Valley School is his to do
with as he sees fit.

Principal George Gallion of Mr. Gallion's
School is concerned about the behavior of Kensington High students, who knock the windows out of
the school and tell teachers what to do. At the
end of Gallion's one year as principal, the students have a different outlook because Gallion
has the raw courage to do what must be done.
Gallion tells John Bennington, one of his teachers,
to be a fighter because people like fighters; as
principal he tells an unreasonable irate parent
to "get the hell out and off of the Hill" of Kensington High;7 during the tremendous free-for-all
between the football fans of Kensington and those
of East Dartmouth, when even women are knocking
each other down, Gallion helps to restore order;
when Lefty Gold Iron, the school's star football
player, swings at Gallion in the principal's office,
the heart-patient administrator K.O.'s the pupil
in knocking him all the way over the office desk.
Still, following graduation ceremonies some parents
want to whip George Gallion for not signing the
senior diplomas of certain students who failed
courses.

In To Teach, To Love Stuart describes the
lifelong battle he has waged for quality education
in Kentucky. As superintendent of Greenup County
Schools, he paid no attention to politicians in
running the school system and he attacked and abol-
ished the ridiculous trustee system. These and
many additional reforms nearly cost Stuart his life
and for a time he left Kentucky education to teach
in Portsmouth, Ohio. Kentucky's greatest educator
has not always been her most popular. In this
novel, Stuart gives a vivid personal account of the
ancient Appalachian tradition of a man's not back-
ing down from a fair fight. When Jesse was an
underclassman at Greenup High, Paul Briswell, a
6' 2", two-hundred pound senior beat him up for no
apparent reason. He blacked both of Stuart's eyes
and knocked him out. Young Jesse trained for the
re-match for weeks in the family smokehouse by
punching a coffee sack filled with seventy pounds
of sand. He also listened to his Uncle Rank's
advice on beginning a fight: "Always get a man
the first lick. That does the work. Hit him hard
too. Stand on your toes and throw your weight

behind your fist. Hit him hard the first time."[8]
Jesse won the rematch.

Stuart's fictional novels present further
examples of violence arising from the Appalachian
subculture's emphasis upon the male as a potentially
explosive individual--ready at all times to take
issue with any slights to his honor. Hie to the
Hunters, repeatedly praised as a classic among
young people's books, begins with sixteen-year-old
Jud Sparks whipping the twin bullies of Greenwood
by spitting ambeer in their eyes and stopping them
from making a punching bag out of the small townboy
Didway Hargis. Jud takes Didway home with him to
the Plum Grove Hills where there is a "war" raging
between fox hunters and tobacco growers. Jud accul-
turates Did over the long summer and early season
of Did's experience as a mountain man, and from
his mountain mentor Did learns to do hard physical
labor, to hunt, to fish, to square dance and to be
well-dressed: to carry a .38 revolver to social
functions. At summer's end Did has muscles on his
arms, color on his cheeks, and the Appalachian
readiness to never again take any 'truck' from
anybody.

Anse Bushman and his son Tarvin of Trees of
Heaven are masterful embodiments of the older Appalachian ethic of male violence. At a square dance
to which Tarvin has taken his beautiful Subrinea,
Tarvin knocks Bollie Beaver "cold as a cucumber"
just as Bollie goes for his pistol, which is notched.
The crowd says the sweeping lick is a "deadner"
and that Tarvin's action proves that people have
not lost the color of their blood; they then throw
the insensate Bollie into the "skimmin hole" (the
pit for catching excess foam from a molasses mill).[9]
Later in the novel, Tarvin and Anse Bushman 'face
down' Lonsey and Bollie Beaver at a public land
auction; both factions are armed with pistols and
they tell the sheriff to stay out of the dispute.

In God's Oddling Stuart recalls a visit as
a youth to his legendary grandfather, Mitch Stuart--
the big timberman of the Big Sandy River country.
Young Jesse was frightened of this man-mountain
who had outworked most horses, drunk whiskey like

88

water, rafted timber on the Big Sandy River, fought
in the Civil War, and waged a lifelong feud with
the Hornbuckles and Dangerfields. As a young man
Stuart attended his grandfather's funeral; feud
enemies had beaten the old man to death.[10]

Early in his life, Jesse chose not to follow
the "fightin Stuart" half of his heritage because
of the fact that violence is never the best solution to human problems. However, in the best
tradition of both the Appalachian and the American
culture, he chose to stand and fight when to flee
would involve betrayal of genuine moral principle
or true honor. Many Stuart short stories reveal
the author's and the Appalachian subculture's
dichotomic attitude toward violence: "Whip-Poor-
Willie," and "The Rightful Owner" are exemplary.
In "Whip-Poor-Willie" a family is ravaged by their
own senseless violence: the father has one eye
knocked out with a rock, one of his sons has an
eye shot out at church and another has both eyes
shot out by his wife.[11] In "The Rightful Owner"
Mick and Shan Powderjay (fictional names for Mick
and Jesse Stuart) are ready to fight it out with
Freeman and Oliver Abdon regarding the ownership
of a stray foxhound the Powderjays have found and
nursed back to excellent form and health. The
Powderjays know that the Abdons will take their
dog if they let them. The dog is not important--
the principle is.[12]

But if the violence inspired by uninhibited
bisexual agressiveness is given its full due by
Stuart, so is its complement, a deep and rewarding
family and sexual love. In the poetry, novels and
short stories of Stuart, the traditional roles of
Appalachian men and women within the family emerge
as a partnership conditioned by life in the Appalachian environment. Stuart has credited the
Appalachian heritage with creating such equality
within the family: "Hard work is our tradition,
too--even for our women. . . . in nearly every
family, the mothers and daughters make clothing
for themselves and others. They make quilts,
curtains, draperies, and rugs for the home. And
when spring comes to the mountains, the young
women, many of whom are high school and college

students and even college graduates, do not think
it is beneath their dignity to work with their
brothers and fathers on the land, riding tractors
in the valleys, setting tobacco by hand, forking
hay, and hoeing in the garden or on the slopes.
It is their heritage."[13]

Throughout the Appalachian subculture and the
entire literary production of Jesse Stuart, the
touchstone, the one fixed mark of all sexually
defined roles, is love--the love of true lovers,
the love of parents and children. The ideal love
of lovers is the romantic pledging of truth between
man and woman. The ideal parental-child love is
unflagging loyalty and concern. Stuart does not
falsify reality. His work depicts prostitution,
homosexuality, child abandonment, and promiscuity,
a full measure of deviant behavior. But the norm
is always the tenderness and respect generated by
the Appalachian family, a society of rugged individuals with a great capacity for loving.

True love does exist in the world and Jesse
Stuart paints it in bold strokes on a proportionate
space of his literary canvas, and his work is
greater for it. Tarvin Bushman and Subrinea
Tussie, Dave and Deutsia Huntoon, are joined by
scores of Stuart lovers whose love is true. Autumn
Lovesong, Stuart's long poem dedicated to his wife
Naomi Deane, depicts his enduring love for his life
companion:

> Knee-deep in leaves, in milkweed furze
>   with sawbrier trimming,
> Your hand in mine to hold,
>   your willowy body leaning
> So your autumn-colored, curly hair is against
>   my face and shoulder:
> So deep in love, in autumn's splendor
>   lucently dying,
> So late in love our autumn is almost over,
> Again we softly kiss, unmindful our time
>   is inexorably going
> To a secret place that is not
>   beyond our knowing.
> . . . .
> . . . .[14]

In like manner, most parents and children do love each other in Stuart's work. Beyond Dark Hills, God's Oddling, The Year of My Rebirth, and numerous short stories and poems reflect Jesse Stuart's great and abiding love for his family. In representative fashion, sonnet 47 of Man With a Bull-Tongue Plow expresses the deep love of a son for his mother:

I shall not speak soft words for her--
my mother.
I shall not praise her to the lofty skies,
But I shall leave her on the earth--
my mother
Would choose the earth in preference to
the skies.
I say the strength of oak is in my mother;
Color of autumn leaves is in my mother
The solidness of hills is in my mother
And in her is the courage of the wind.
And in her is the rain's cool sympathy.
I hope she gives me strength of the oak tree;
I hope she gives me solidness of hills--
This with the strength of twisted grape-vine
will.
I hope she gives me courage of the wind
And backbone that is hard as stone to bend--
I need these things to serve me to the end.

To a greater degree than in the contemporary dominant American culture, there are still constants in the Appalachian world depicted by Jesse Stuart, and perhaps the prime constant is love. The main question of the Appalachian household is not who shall dominate but if the 'long sweetnin' (true love) exists between man and woman. The main question regarding the relationship of parents and children is neither discipline nor the lack of it, but love. In Stuart's world of W-Hollow love is not for sale, it cannot be earned, it cannot be lost, and it is to the death--as ageless and unchanging as the Appalachian mountains. Stuart's literary embodiment of such love is one of his major fortes as a creative artist.

NOTES

1. Harry M. Caudill, *Night Comes to the Cumber-lands* (Boston: Little, Brown, 1962), p. 45.

2. "Greenup Poet," *Time*, 7 Nov. 1938, p. 63.

3. Stanley J. Kunitz and Howard Haycraft, eds., *Twentieth Century Authors* (New York: The H. W. Wilson Co., 1942), p. 6.

4. Jesse Stuart, *Man With a Bull-Tongue Plow* (New York: E. P. Dutton, 1934), p. 34.

5. Jesse Stuart, *Album of Destiny* (New York: E. P. Dutton, 1944), p. 188.

6. Jesse Stuart, *Beyond Dark Hills* (New York: E. P. Dutton, 1938), p. 158.

7. Jesse Stuart, *Mr. Gallion's School* (New York: McGraw-Hill, 1967), p. 120.

8. Jesse Stuart, *To Teach, To Love* (New York: The World Publishing Company, 1970), pp. 59-61.

9. Jesse Stuart, *Trees of Heaven* (New York: E. P. Dutton, 1940), pp. 65-77.

10. Jesse Stuart, *God's Oddling* (New York: McGraw-Hill, 1960), pp. 121-128.

11. Jesse Stuart, *Men of the Mountains* (New York: E. P. Dutton, 1941), pp. 283-302.

12. Jesse Stuart, *My Land Has A Voice* (New York: McGraw Hill, 1966), pp. 159-172.

13. Jesse Stuart, "Ascend the High Mountain," *Country Beautiful*, Feb. 1962, pp. 14-15.

14. Jesse Stuart, *Autumn Lovesong* (Kansas City, Missouri: Hallmark Cards, 1971), p. 5.

CHAPTER SIX

RECREATION OR PLAY

Among the dark hills of Jesse Stuart's literary world, one is never at too great a distance from laughter--a great deal of laughter. The dark side of human existence is no more prevalent in Stuart's works than the winter is in his mountains. A great deal of Stuart's humor arises from his honest depiction of the original Appalachian form of recreation, the traditional Scotch-Irish love of kidding, debating, and fighting over any aspect of religion, liquor, or politics. A sampling of Stuart's claimants to the one true mountain faith includes The Church of the New Faith, The Church of The Old Faith, Methodists, Baptists, Free Will Baptists, Foot Washing Baptists, and Forty Gallon Baptists. The booze is moonshine whiskey and the politics is Democrat or Republican. To be "right" in both the Appalachian subculture and in Stuart's depiction of that subculture often means that one attends the same church building, holds the same attitude toward the consumption of alcohol, and is a member of the same political party as the person doing the classifying.

To understand and appreciate Stuart's and the Appalachian subculture's employment of religious themes for humorous effect, it is necessary to know something of the religious heritage of Appalachia. The religious background of the rest of the United States--i.e. the Puritanism of New England, the Quakerism of Pennsylvania, the Anglicanism of Virginia, the Irish Catholicism of Boston, the Lutheranism of the Midwest, and the traditional Catholicism and Judaism of large and growing American cities--has not been shared by Appalachia:[1] "the first settlers in Appalachia, who came largely from the lower economic groups, were a diverse lot religiously--Scotch Presbyterians, English Puritans and Separatists, and nonconforming sectarians from various backgrounds. No one church ever developed sufficient strength to draw them together. People were too widely separated and travel was too

difficult for a stable ministry to be provided.
Trained clergymen on the east coast, already over-
burdened with the press of the fast-growing population there, were reluctant to travel into the
untamed wilds of Appalachia."[2]

These frontier conditions produced lay
preachers in a situation wherein every man became
a prophet, recognizing no religious authority but
himself. Following the great religious revivals
which swept through Appalachia during the 1800's,
many Appalachians formed their own churches, built
their own buildings and ordained each other as
reverends.[3]

Following the Civil War, religious fundamen-
talism of the most literal sort flourished in
Appalachia. The King James Bible was believed
literally and preached by men untrained and unlearned in theology who had felt a divine summons
to proclaim the word of God; they preached a basic
form of Calvinism imported from Scotland.[4] In this
Appalachian religious environment, the Bible has
been and is looked upon as a magical book but it
is read little. The evolved result is a folk
religion based upon "sentiment, tradition, super-
stition, and personal feelings, all reinforcing
the patterns of the culture."[5]

Throughout the history of Appalachia there
has thus been no sense of community provided by
organized religion and a priesthood, and during
modern times only twelve to fifteen percent of the
population are church members or affiliated with
churches.[6] And it has been truly said that the
church in Appalachia has been the most reactionary
force in the mountains:[7] "Through a century-and-
three quarters the mountaineers, in the main, have
stayed remarkably irreligious. They simply are
not joiners, spurning organizations of any kind
except the political parties. They have retained
a respected reverence for the Holy Bible and for
the Protestant cause but it is a reverence without scholarship, discipline or leadership. When
religion comes it is usually with advancing age
or as the result of some highly traumatic emotional
experience. With the return of health or better

times there is a strong likelihood the convert will 'backslide.' Much, indeed most, religion comes with the shadow of the deathbed."[8]

Many of Jesse Stuart's characters, like those of Mark Twain, simply have no "truck" with organized religion, and God is not viewed as a kindly "paterfamilias" who will come some day to lead them kindly home. Anice Bealer, hard-working father of nine children, never goes to church but spends his Sundays walking in God's green woods. He does sell land and cattle to his neighbors on credit, without bank notes, because they always pay him back. His philosophy is live and let live.[9] Lima Whittengill believes that life is, after all, a joke. Resurrection Morn never comes and man lives once and then never again.[10] As a young boy, Jesse Stuart thought that God hid behind trees and waited to hit him with a stick.[11]

Stuart's tongue-in-cheek examination of the many "one true faith" mountain religions provides much of his human comedy. God and the Devil have many fights at the Plum Grove Church where men outside the church come to shoot, drink, and fight with knives and razors, while people inside wrestle with the flesh, the spirit and the sermon. Typical of Stuart's fictional mountain literalists are Brother Dusty of the Holiness Faith Healers, who preached that Hell was nineteen miles straight under the ground;[12] Peter Leadingham, a Forty Gallon Baptist, who thinks that Heaven is a mile or two above his head;[13] and Reverend Ezekiel Wrenhouse, a Forty Gallon Baptist minister, who was forced to leave the mountains because he beat up and was shot by another preacher who argued for sprinkling converts rather than "sousing them under."[14]

The fate of those Stuart characters who question mountain literalism is exemplified in Op Aker's narrative of Brother Adjer, who did exactly that with a flair for the dramatic. Brother Adjer appeared at the church door dressed in long hair and flowing robes to see if the congregation, who had been praying for just such a happening, really did want Jesus to come down through a hole in the roof-- after the stampede, there was no one left to satisfy his curiosity. This experiment ruined his reputation and forced him to move to Oklahoma.[15] The drunken Uncle Jeff suffers a similar religious and social ostracism and is thrown in jail for telling a church congregation that it would be impractical and expensive for God to answer their fervent prayer and tear off the shingles and enter the church through the roof.[16]

The narrow doctrinal intolerance of countless Appalachian Protestant splinter-groups is humorously reflected in a kind of cosmic Stuart irony which leads one to question doctrinal intolerance in all religions. Anse Maddox, a Forty Gallon Baptist who sees no harm in drinking liquor, wonders if it would be permissible for him to date a beautiful and most heavenly endowed preacher of the Unknown Tongue who allows no whiskey and tobacco in her Valhalla.[17] Similarly, the two young lovers of "Love in the Spring" are "doctrine-crossed" because a Slab Baptist, who drinks 'licker,' bets on chicken fights and plays cards, is an infidel to a shouting Methodist.[18] All pleasures of the world are denied to Thomas Bowling by his Church of the Old Faith and its moderator Egbert Chanute. Thomas has heeded his faith's admonition that the Devil lurks at Coney Island, Churchill Downs and in his own hometown at Blakesburg's Hilldale Theater. As a true penitent he has denied himself horse races, movies, circuses, tobacco, whiskey, and the funnies--all to no avail; he is "churched" (expelled) for buying a television set.[19]

In Stuart's work, as in the Appalachian subculture, this narrow doctrinal intolerance does not necessarily end at the grave. When Grandpa Radner is buried, the family relatives of The Old Faith and The New Faith have a free-for-all in the graveyard. At issue is the proper place of Grandpa's grave site and the donnybrook lasts nearly an hour. All these Christian soldiers are so badly beaten and exhausted that they decide to leave the old man where he is.[20]

Jesse Stuart's land of doctrinal intolerance is inevitably the land of "weaked (wicked) water," and attitudes toward the consumption of alcohol

permeate all aspects of Appalachian culture. Too
often the attitude toward alcohol permits only two
possibilities—total abstinence or the consumption
of enough whiskey to float saw logs down the Big
Sandy. Perhaps only in Appalachia is man's fate
"bourbon crossed."

There is a fount that flows in the works of
Stuart but not from God. Like Saint John in the
wilderness, Op Akers has visions, but they arise
from his periodic communion with homemade persimmon
brandy, which Op carries on fox hunts. Op partakes
until he is senseless and lies exposed to the
elements of his high ridge country; he awakes in
the morning with rain water collected on his eye-
lids and memories of riding the great hairy back
of the Evil One during the previous night's thunder
storm.[21]

Stuart presents many unforgettable portraits
of "poor damned souls" who drink excessively.
Bird Neck, a seventy-nine-year-old farmer, declares
that after three wives his fourth wife is two
gallons of moonshine whiskey. He boasts that when
young he could drink a gallon a day and work, dance
and foxhunt, and that he once drank five quarts
and lay "beyond speech" in the hot July sun with
lizards running and playing over his body.[22]
Another great drinker who staggers through Stuart's
work is the notorious Uncle Jeff Hilton. His
Powderjay nephews may discover him in the company
of two gallons—singing under a rock cliff,[23] or
they may be forced by their mother to take mule
and sled and fetch the slumbering, insensate,
cow-dung besmirched Gulliver home from a neighbor's
barn where he has been on a week-long drunk—
sipping moonshine from straws stuck in gallon
jugs.[24]

Many of Stuart's men of the jug enjoy an
adoptive second family, a friendly neighborhood
bar, and a home away from home at the shack of
the notorious moonshine brewers, Sylvania and
Skinny, whose product carries the hallmark of
making its users "drunk as a biled (boiled) owl."
The diminutive Skinny is married to the gargantuan
Sylvania, who weighs 650 pounds and has not been

out of the house since she was a little girl; the
"Revenooers" can do nothing with her since they
cannot remove her from her house through any door
or window. She has been a mother to all the men
customers who act as pallbearers on her funeral
day and remove her body from the shack by tearing
down the chimney.[25]

Several Stuart characters make a treaty of
conditional amnesty with God, and they give up
the drinking of "weaked waters" when near the
point of death. Two years before his death Battle
Keaton quits drinking, joins the church, and makes
his peace with God; he will not, however, forget
the Turners--his feud enemies.[26] In a deathbed
confession Mel Renfro makes his peace with God
and with his moonshine partner Cief Salyers. Mel
confesses to killing three revenue agents and
making love to Cief's wife. Cief says that if
Mel had any chance in getting well, he would "blow
his goddamned brains out."[27]

In portraying this strange Appalachian admix-
ture of narrow sectarianism, individual interpretation of Holy Writ, and alcohol, Jesse Stuart is
never condescending toward his characters nor does
he pass judgment upon their world view. Rather,
he consistently maintains that compassionate and
disinterested viewpoint which is the hallmark of
all major literary artists, and there is no
"typical" Stuart character who embodies the Appalachian religious concepts. In their daily lives,
many Stuart characters, as he has described his
parents, live a type of Christianity that is as
old as the carpenter from Nazareth and his elite
crowd of simple laborers and fishermen:"Mom and
Dad didn't pretend their Christianity, nor wear
it on Sunday clothes. They lived it, taught it."[28]

Politics and the law are two other rich mines
of humor for Stuart and recreation for his Appalachians. Only recently has the dominant American
culture come to adopt an attitude toward the
inequality of law enforcement and toward politicians that has been traditional in Appalachia.
In the dominant culture this disillusionment with
due process and the honesty of politicians has

arisen as a result of mass media revelations that
those in high places rarely face the letter of the
law. In Stuart's honest literary embodiment of
the Appalachian subculture, mistrust of legal
officials can be attributed to inequalities under
the law in Scotland and Ireland in the eighteenth
century and after the massive immigration to
America and migration to the Appalachian mountains.

Whiskey enters into this aspect of Appalachian life as well. These Scotsmen and Irishmen
brought a knowledge of distilling to the Blue
Ridge where they learned to substitute Indian corn
for the rye and barley of the Old World. In Kentucky they sold their legal cash-crop in Frankfort
or Louisville, and in other smaller settlement
towns they sold whiskey to other distilling elements. With the later development of the coal-field
towns, a bushel of corn valued at $1.00 could be
converted to whiskey and sold for $30.00 to $40.00
per gallon.[29]

Prohibition and the period 1920-1934 brought
the Moonshine War. This period witnessed the massive development of both big city and local trade;
the hauling of hidden moonshine in automobiles,
trucks and coal cars; the incarceration of many
Appalachians in the federal penitentiaries at
Atlanta and Leavensworth; and a shooting war in
which thirty-five agents were killed in Kentucky
alone. In this bloody battle many moonshiners
custom-loaded their shells with chopped-off
nailheads and screws and fired them from 12, 10
and 8 gauge shotguns. Kentucky gubernatorial
pardons for moonshine killers of powerful family
connections were prevalent during the "war":
"The double standards of the Prohibition era had
a profound impact on the mind and character of
the mountaineer. Realizing that he was being
pilloried by a society for manufacturing a product
which that same society demanded and highly prized,
he developed an abiding distrust of officials at
all levels. He became deeply suspicious of the
motives of government, both state and Federal, and
cynical of its purposes in every field."[30]

Official corruption, particularly this

inequality in enforcing the laws against moonshining, helped cause both Appalachians and Stuart's Appalachian characters to mistrust law officers and politicians. The issue and consequences can be extremely serious for the individuals involved, but spiting and circumventing the law is one of the keenest delights in the Appalachian world.

Charlie Splean and other personas of Man With A Bull-Tongue Plow are Appalachian embodiments of mistrust of the law and legal officials. Charlie "works like hell and hates the goddamn law." He is frequently jailed for drunkenness and his father has paid enough fines to buy Charlie a hundred-acre farm:

> But we have got too goddamn many laws
> I've never tried to do my neighbors harm,
> And yet I've laid behind stone walls and
> bars. (33)

Jim Long, serving a penitentiary sentence for moonshining, is homesick for the winds and fields of home and wonders about the justice of his Uncle Sam who paid an informer $50.00 to spy on him:

> Why is it wrong for men to run a still?
> Now Uncle Sam's stool-pigeons sell and buy,
> And money is their God--their only cry. (45)

Jim plans to kill the informer. The persona of sonnet 249 must leave the hills and whiskey making because he shot a revenue agent dressed like a farmer. The hardworking farmer of sonnet 66 must sell moonshine and tobacco to clothe his fourteen children, and he prays nightly that the wolf of hunger will be kept from his door.

In Hie to the Hunters Stuart depicts many of the discrepancies between the dominant American culture and the Appalachian subculture in their differing attitudes and behavior toward the law of the land. The runaway townboy, Didway Hargis, who lives in the Plum Grove Hills with Jud Sparks and his mountain parents, Peg and Arn, for a few months, comes to understand the Appalachian atti-

100

tude toward the law when Jud explains to Did that Cief Eversole is a polecat who makes $25.00 "fer turnin a man over to the revenooers" while Cief makes whiskey himself.[31]

Such characters as Anse Bushman (T O H), Don Praytor (D O L), Kim Tussie (T F P T) and a young abandoned invalid girl in the short story "Fern" also embody the Appalachian attitude that law and justice are not necessarily the same thing. Anse Bushman maintains that Greenwood lawsuits never settle anything and at their conclusion guns begin to crack and powder and lead decide.[32] Don Praytor knows that justice is a different thing for those who live back in the high mountains than for those living in valleys and towns: "I'd stayed in that goddamned jail until Id've rotted and I wouldn't 've got a trial, he said. I told you why they kept me there. Money for that son-of-bitch o' a jailor. There's no justice for a man from this mountain."[33] When Kim Tussie returns home from World War II, the only thing that keeps him from killing his great-uncle George, who has just shot and killed Kim's brother Mott, is the fact that George leaves the back door more quickly than Kim can enter the front.[34] All of these and many additional Stuart characters would agree with the justice-outside-the-law attitude of the narrator of "Fern" regarding the justice that should be dealt to the legal guardians of an invalid young girl, who abandoned her to slowly starve and to freeze to death in a mountain shack: "Hell's too good for such people. That's why we have powder and lead and plowlines and trees."[35]

Because of this dichotomy in the attitude of the Appalachian subculture toward law and justice, Jesse Stuart has said that a Greenup County deputy sheriff jailing men from the ridges faces men who would make television western characters seem like angels.[36] Stuart's fictional law officers provide ample testimony to the truth of his statement.

Even though they hold an indisputable advantage in firepower, Sheriff Watkins is a little less than anxious to lead his small brigade of Greenbriar deputies back into the mountains to

capture the old and crazy patriarch of a large
club-swinging clan--Zeke Hammertight. Sheriff
Watkins builds his courage by thinking of his
superior arsenal and picturing himself as George
Washington or Teddy Roosevelt in the certain
approaching donnybrook--"the battle of the bresh
(brush)": "You know a double-barrel shotgun
shooting number-three shots with black powder is
better than fifteen clubs, five pitchforks, ten
garden hoes, five brier scythes, and a half-dozen
double-bitted axes."[37]

Federal agent Keaton Battlestrife matches
wits with and finally captures Eif Cluggish, Blake
County's richest moonshine maker, in "Evidence is
High Proof," a short story that brilliantly embodies the ancient hound-fox Appalachian game of
agent versus distiller. Eif owns the biggest
dairy in Tibert River Valley and uses his business
to mask his moonshine, which he sells for $40.00
per gallon. He rides Thunderbolt, the fastest
horse in Blake County, and looks with pride at his
twenty-three mule teams and wagons loaded with
'supplies.' Eif's drivers are loyal and will fight
for him, and he fears only Keaton Battlestrife--
an agent who will not "hook up with" any local
political faction. Keaton is embarrassed when he
falsely arrests Eif for hauling milk. Refusing
to be laughed out of Appalachia, he so closely
pursues Eif and Eif's son one winter night that
they must plunge their horses into and ford a
river, and he finally arrests Eif by mastering
Eif's signal system and relaying the all-clear
on a night swarming with agents.[38]

Without the voluntary help and instruction
provided by members of the Appalachian subculture,
neither local nor federal officers have any
effectiveness in enforcing the law, which the
Appalachian, because of experience, interprets
not as impersonal but as politically oriented.
In this light Stuart's "The Moonshine War" provides insights to members of the dominant culture
regarding a type of Appalachian legal-political
inequality of which they perhaps are little aware.

The town of Argill in Greenwood County,

102

Kentucky, consists of "a store, post office, two filling stations and a Methodist church where, maybe, two dozen people attend every Sunday." Argill has the reputation of selling whiskey by the gallon jug and horse quart (Texas fifth), and the Argill moonshining is the family enterprise of "the Big Four in Moonshining": the Caudells, the Whaleys, the Fortners, and the Luttrells. As a result of a particularly sobering revival, the heads of the four families join the local church and give up the moonshine business. The reader learns much from Chris Caudell and his older brother. Chris functioned as a lookout for his father's illegal distilling operation and when "the Law" was in the area he warned his father by three toots on a foxhorn; the periodic destruction of his father's unattended still made big news in the <u>Greenwood</u> <u>County</u> <u>Gazette</u>. Following their father's reformation, the Caudell brothers must buy their moonshine in the men's room of the Greenwood County Courthouse--"the safe place to buy"--from Pegleg Joe Radner, who wears an overcoat, winter and summer, filled with pints.[39]

Rendering unto God and unto Caesar is a reality in Appalachia and in Stuart's fictional and poetic portrayal of that area. Mick Powderjay and his old friend Flem Simpson know they will be mountain Republican and mountain Democrat after burial.[40] Both Mick and Shan Powderjay know that it is not amusing to be a Republican in Kentucky, and Shan must fight his Democratic classmates and teacher for survival.[41] But because of partiality in the enforcement of the law and the meddling of corrupt officials, Stuart's Appalachians do not respect either law enforcement officers or politicians.

A whole gallery of poetic personas in M W B-T P express the Appalachian disdain for those who enforce the law for their own advantage. The farmer of sonnet 340 voices the general Appalachian evaluation of the law and the politician: "I hate the law--God damn the politician." The honest voter of sonnet 276, who refuses offered bribes, challenges crooked state politicians to a public brawl and calls them "God-damned crooked sticks"

and "green parasitic flies" which cling to dung.
Sonnets 421 and 422 depict the Appalachian esti-
mate of the office of constable. A constable is
too despicable for "mountain men to touch when he
is dead," and a dead constable, shot while snoop-
ing in the hills for moonshine stills, should be
left for hounds and "piss-ants" to bury.

Plowing farmers in sonnet 273 hear the distant county courthouse bells calling men to justice
and they wonder about that "justice":

> They say: "We've done no harm that we
> can see.
> We make our living from these sprouty
> hills.
> Our money goes to pay a lawyer's fee
> Because we operate our moonshine
> stills. . . ."

Observing a session of courthouse justice, the
persona of sonnet 274 describes the place as one
of the world's most wretched places, "the hell-
house of poor devils," where lawyers prosecute
poor men for such offenses as intent to kill,
making love in the weeds, and the possession of
moonshine stills:

> Lawyers arise and make their speal
> and splash.
> Poor wretches bow their heads and
> cuss the pen
> (For laws are hard when men don't
> have the cash);

The personas of sonnets 639 and 640 extend
the same quality of mercy to a dead judge and
jailer, who are weary of the narrow confines of
their earthen cells, as these officials extended
to living men. The persona of sonnet 639 tells
Judge Winthrop that the judge must forever listen
to the sound of his own gavel pounding on his
grave because in life the judge sent many good
and honest farmers to the penitentiary for making
whiskey:

"That is your gavel, Judge Winthrop,
The one you used for order in the room—
The one you used when many met their doom.
. . . .
Now lie there, Judge, this is your final
doom—
The gavel, Judge—it's order in the room!"

The persona of sonnet 640 extends the same letter-
of-the-law mercy to dead Jailer Dave Barnes who
has grown exceedingly weary of being shut behind
"Earth's heavy jail-house doors": "Lie there
forever—damn your dust to hell!"

In all of Stuart's work perhaps the epitome
of injustice is found in sonnet 112 of M W B-T P
wherein the persona describes the death of a brave
Plum Grove lad. A fugitive from a jail sentence,
the young man is ambushed by brave law officers
at night. He returns fire in the direction of the
trees where they are hiding and he flees, holding
his fingers over two holes of spurting blood so
they cannot track him in the leaves. He rests
upon a bed of thick leaves with a white sand-stone
pillow and dies before morning:

Next day country newspapers thus read:
"Murderer Escapes Left Two Policemen Dead."

It is no accident that Stuart's lifetime work
is filled with satirical and humorous portraits of
corrupt politicians and highly circumspect election
practices. Politics is another of Appalachia's
national pastimes. In 1974 Stuart collected the
best of these short stories proving beyond reason-
able doubt that "Kentucky politics are the damndest."
The characters who perform their Machiavellian
chicanery in 32 Votes Before Breakfast rank squarely
with Mark Twain's Duke and Dauphin as some of the
greatest and funniest rogues in American literature.
Anyone who would charge Stuart with any degree of
exaggeration in portraying his political scamps
has only to experience the highly different and
festive world of an Applachian election day.

Uncle Casper in his bid for the state senate

promises better roads, schools, and two hams in
every smokehouse for those who vote "on the Lord's
side"; Casper also promises to provide feather
beds for drunks (2-3). Senator Foulfoot literally
eats himself into an early grave and none of his
political cronies attends his funeral (63-64).
Mose Winthrop, the herb (moonshine) king of Kentucky, passes himself off as Governor Randall
Spoon of Kentucky during the annual excursion of
his patrons to a Chicago ball game. He looks like
a governor and he makes an inspiring twenty-minute
speech to a Richmond, Indiana, audience (78-86).

32 Votes Before Breakfast is dedicated "to
the winners and losers, Republicans and Democrats
(called, in this book, Little Party and Big Party
and Greenoughs and Dinwiddies)--the most colorful,
intriguing and fascinating men of any profession,
who battled with no holds barred to win public
offices in county, state and national elections"
(VII). The Appalachian politicians of this collection of short stories use the laws of the land
only to further their own ends and defeat the
opposite political party.

Mr. Silas Devers, a vote hauler of great
stature for the Greenough Party, attempts the
undreamed of feat of attempting to vote a man,
under various assumed local names, in all thirty-
two precincts of Blake County. He pays a young
man named Dave ten dollars to chauffeur and the
smooth-talking Al Caney two dollars per successful
vote. Guzzling Mr. Dever's 'election whiskey,'
Al becomes increasingly more bold and righteously
indignant as his right to vote is successively
questioned. At Blakesburg Precinct No. 2,
Mr. Devers makes the fatal mistake of telling
Al to vote as the Reverend Spencer Hix, a prominent
local minister who has just voted and is sitting
in his car outside the polls. Al is too intoxicated
to back down and declares to the poll officials,
"I've voted twenty-eight times for the Greenoughs,
and I aim to vote again." After being attacked by
three election officials and a parasol-wielding
matron, Mr. Devers and Dave flee the maelstrom.

Jesse Stuart powerfully satirizes the narrow-mindedness which tolerates such flagrant abuses of American democracy, and he effectively holds up to ridicule the paradox of the constituent loyalty of those who continually vote for politicians who neither understand nor work for the welfare of their citizenry. One of Stuart's prosecuting attorneys dismisses a charge of "breaking and entering and robbery" against Erric Pratt, a member of the nine-family Pratt clan, because Erric did not break into a store but entered through a hole in the roof. The Pratts admit they were wrong in thinking the boy would be sent to prison; they had underestimated their own influence: "Eighty-one votes is more than money in our county and state. . . . Eighty-one votes is wealth" (230-231).

In one short story Stuart maintains that even the scientific community is baffled as to how politicians who serve only their own interests can continue to receive unflagging loyalty from their automaton constituents. Following the death of Congressman Rothwell Periwinkle (Big Party), there is a Blakesburg rumor that the Honorable Rothwell was so heavily in debt following fourteen successive terms as a high-living United States congressman that he had to fake his own funeral and sell his body to science in order to avoid total financial ruin. Scientists supposedly want to study the brain of a politician who could hold his constituents in the palm of his hand (57).

Stuart's Appalachian characters--who inhabit his land of the one true faith, of "weaked" waters, of unequal justice under the "goddamn law," and of scallywag politicians--live in mutually exclusive territories, and this understood exclusiveness provides much of the daily humor of Appalachians. A Forty Gallon Baptist and a Methodist, a constable and a moonshiner, and a Greenough and a Dinwiddie-- all superficially have little use for one another and are the butt of each other's jokes and often very rough kidding. However, in the case of real human need or of death, Jesse Stuart's apparently uncompromising hillmen lay aside these various sectarian masks and become brothers: "There is

107

something to human beings--a strange something. They fight each other and kill in the mountains but in a case of death they stand side by side, solid as the hills for each other with chains of friendship eternity cannot break."[42]

NOTES

1. Jack E. Weller, <u>Yesterday's People</u> (Lexington, Ky.: University of Kentucky Press, 1965), p. 122.

2. Earl D. C. Brewer, "Religion and the Churches," in <u>The Southern Appalachian Region: A Survey</u>, ed. by Thomas R. Ford (Lexington, Ky.: University of Kentucky Press, 1962), p. 201, in <u>Yesterday's People</u>, pp. 122-123.

3. Weller, <u>Yesterday's People</u>, pp. 123-126.

4. Harry M. Caudill, <u>Night Comes to the Cumberlands</u> (Boston: Little, Brown, 1962), pp. 56-57.

5. Weller, <u>Yesterday's People</u>, pp. 130-131.

6. Caudill, <u>Night Comes to the Cumberlands</u>, p. 58.

7. Weller, <u>Yesterday's People</u>, p. 126.

8. Caudill, <u>Night Comes to the Cumberlands</u>, p. 349.

9. Jesse Stuart, <u>Man With a Bull-Tongue Plow</u> (New York: E. P. Dutton, 1934), pp. 245-246.

10. Ibid., 279.

11. Jesse Stuart, <u>Beyond Dark Hills</u> (New York: E. P. Dutton, 1938), p. 74.

12. Jesse Stuart, <u>Daughter of the Legend</u> (New York: McGraw-Hill, 1965), p. 83.

13. Jesse Stuart, <u>Tales From the Plum Grove Hills</u> (New York: E. P. Dutton, 1946), p. 249.

14. Jesse Stuart, <u>Come Back to the Farm</u> (New York: McGraw Hill, 1971), p. 154.

15. Jesse Stuart, <u>The Good Spirit of Laurel Ridge</u> (New York: McGraw-Hill, 1956), p. 163.

16. Jesse Stuart, Plowshare in Heaven (New York: McGraw-Hill, 1956), p. 163.

17. Jesse Stuart, Head O' W-Hollow (New York: E. P. Dutton, 1936), pp. 105-109.

18. Jesse Stuart, Come Gentle Spring (New York: McGraw-Hill, 1969), pp. 64-65.

19. Stuart, Plowshare in Heaven, pp. 254-261.

20. Ibid., 225-226.

21. Stuart, The Good Spirit of Laurel Ridge, pp. 214-219.

22. Stuart, Plowshare in Heaven, pp. 173-177.

23. Jesse Stuart, God's Oddling (New York: McGraw-Hill, 1960), p. 104.

24. Jesse Stuart, My Land Has A Voice (New York: McGraw-Hill, 1966), p. 175.

25. Stuart, Plowshare in Heaven, pp. 74-81.

26. Stuart, Tales From the Plum Grove Hills, pp. 174, 191.

27. Stuart, Clearing in the Sky, pp. 43-45.

28. Jesse Stuart, The Year of My Rebirth (New York: McGraw-Hill, 1956), p. 31.

29. Caudill, Night Comes to the Cumberlands, pp. 20, 21, 36, 123.

30. Ibid., 153-162, 164.

31. Jesse Stuart, Hie to the Hunters (New York: McGraw-Hill, 1950), p. 84.

32. Jesse Stuart, Trees of Heaven (New York: E. P. Dutton, 1940), p. 332.

33. Stuart, Daughter of the Legend, p. 68.

34. Jesse Stuart, _Taps for Private Tussie_ (New York: The World Publishing Company, 1969), pp. 292-293.

35. Jesse Stuart, _Men of the Mountains_ (New York: E. P. Dutton, 1941), p. 203.

36. Jesse Stuart, _A Jesse Stuart Reader_ (New York: McGraw-Hill, 1963), p. 83.

37. Stuart, _Plowshare in Heaven_, p. 21.

38. Stuart, _Clearing in the Sky_, pp. 219-227.

39. Jesse Stuart, _32 Votes Before Breakfast_ (New York: McGraw Hill, 1974), pp. 29-44.

40. Stuart, _Men of the Mountains_, p. 26.

41. Stuart, _Tales From the Plum Grove Hills_, p. 250.

42. Stuart, _Men of the Mountains_, p. 204.

Jesse Stuart during recovery period
of first heart attack, June 28, 1955

CHAPTER SEVEN

EDUCATION

> Faces were against the windowpanes and
> many pupils waved jubilantly to us as
> we rode by, our coat-tails riding the
> wind behind our saddles, and the ends
> of our scarfs bright banners on the
> wind. We rode victoriously down the
> main street of Landsburgh on our way
> home.
>
> /Jesse Stuart and his six Tiber Valley
> mountain students departing on their
> seventeen-mile mule journey home after
> defeating a city-county school of nearly
> 400 pupils in a scholastic contest--
> The Thread That Runs So True (101)._/

As previous chapters have shown, Jesse Stuart
is abundantly aware of acculturation, the informal
pattern by which older members of a culture pass
on their ways to the younger generation. Stuart
himself is a product of that informal educational
process, and he demonstrates its workings throughout his literary production. But this chapter is
about the impact of formal schooling on Stuart's
life and work and about his views on the problems
of education in Appalachia. Education is so much
a part of Jesse Stuart that it is an open question
whether he is a writer who teaches or a teacher
who writes. So much of his life has been spent
as a student, teacher, school administrator,
educational prophet, and apologist for learning
that his experiences in these roles have indelibly
stamped his entire literary output, making education one of his most universal themes and leaving
him perhaps the most committed defender of learning
in the history of American literature.

During the tumultuous period of the 1960's,
Robert F. Kennedy made a speech to students at

Alice Lloyd College encouraging them to remain
in eastern Kentucky and use their precious gift
of a college education to help their fellow Appalachians: "You are the most exclusive minority
in the world. Very, very few citizens of the
world have a college education. And with training
comes responsibility to help others. . . . You can
make a difference. One person fighting for his
people, his community, his state, his cause can
make a difference."[1]

Long before and in the years following
Kennedy's speech, Jesse Stuart practiced Kennedy's
advice that the educated Appalachian should remain
with his people and use his precious gift of education, the only real key to solving the problems
both of Appalachia and of American society:

But the greatest poverty we have here,
and in other parts of America, is the
poverty of the mind. If we didn't have
poverty of the mind, we wouldn't have
poverty of the stomach. And there are
those beyond Appalachia who think the
only thing to do with Appalachian youth
(especially the boys) is to give them
vocational training and send them off to
industrial plants and factories in the
North. . . . .
People of Appalachia are not dumb.
They are not trained in comparison with
youth outside of Appalachia who have
better schools and better everything.
Give the youth of Appalachia now better
educational opportunities to eliminate
poverty of the mind. Train their minds
and their hands and in a very short time
Appalachia will move upwards to new
heights."[2]

In Stuart's literary embodiment of the Appalachian subculture, there is no middle ground
regarding the importance of schooling. Fortunately
for Appalachian education and for American literature , the Stuart family cast their lot solidly on
the side of the schools, and Jesse Stuart has
truly become a majority of one as one of America's

greatest living educators and writers about the American educational process.

Neither of Stuart's parents had an elementary education, but they both realized the value of learning and encouraged their children to obtain an education: "They both believed in school. Mother hung our A's up on the wall. She told us we were good, and we believed it. She'd always say to us, 'I want people to see you on the streets of Greenup and say, "There's Martha Hylton's son!"' Now how can you fail a woman like that?"[3]

Beyond Dark Hills, The Thread That Runs So True, Mr. Gallion's School, and To Teach To Love are the four autobiographical novels depicting Stuart's battle on behalf of education. All four books depict Stuart's experiences as a student and as a professional educator, but the focus of each of these four great novels is different. From reading them one comes to an appreciation of Jesse Stuart as one of Appalachia's and America's greatest educators--a man who has made a difference in his lifetime as a result of his education odyssey from Plum Grove to the world.

Jesse walked to the Plum Grove elementary school where he was greatly influenced by Calvin Clarke, a man who taught all eight grades in a one-room school. Because of the short school term and the fact that Jesse had to frequently miss school to help the family make a living, by the age of fifteen Jesse had only approximately twenty-two months of schooling when he decided to enter Greenup High School and was accepted on the basis of qualifying examinations. He walked the five miles to and from high school where he was greatly influenced by his English teacher, Mrs. R. E. Hatton, who encouraged all her students to write well.

Following high school, Stuart worked for one year in a carnival and at the steel mills in Ashland, Kentucky, before entering Lincoln Memorial University in Harrogate, Tennessee. At Lincoln Memorial he worked half days and graduated with a B average. He was particularly devoted to one English professor, Harry Harrison Kroll, an author who encouraged his students to write creatively.

Following graduation Stuart returned home and taught the fourteen students of Winston High School, where he was the entire faculty. His efforts were so successful there that he was offered and accepted the principalship of Greenup High School. After an outstanding academic year for Greenup High, Stuart requested and was refused a modest raise. The following year he entered Vanderbilt University for a year of graduate work under circumstances that would have stopped most men in those hard years of the depression.

At Vanderbilt Jesse worked half days in the cafeteria and was one of only two student janitors. During the first part of his year there, he lived on eleven meals per week and at the end of the year he existed on one meal a day. A fire near the end of the year destroyed all his clothes, many of his poems, and his work on his Masters thesis; however, he finished the term.

Following his year at Vanderbilt, Stuart returned to his father's home in W-Hollow for a year of farm work and great poetic output; he could find no other job at this time. At the age of twenty-four, he was then offered and accepted the position as Superintendent of Greenup County schools--the youngest Superintendent in the history of Kentucky.

As superintendent, Stuart was responsible for many needed reforms in the Greenup County school system and many of his friends and his enemies advised him to step down. He accepted the principalship of McKell High School and during his four years of teaching there he did graduate work at Peabody College in Nashville to make himself a better teacher and McKell a model school.

After his years at McKell High School, Stuart received a Guggenheim Fellowship and traveled in England, Scotland and twenty-seven European countries. Returning home, he married a fellow-teacher, Naomi Norris, a girl with whom he had attended Greenup High School. Jesse and Naomi settled down

116

in their present home in W-Hollow, and Jesse tried
to make a living by sheep-farming and writing;
however, he lost too many sheep to dogs and eventually accepted the position as Superintendent of
Greenup City Schools.

During World War II Stuart was an officer in
the United States Navy and served as a member of
a corps of writers. Following World War II, the
Stuarts returned to W-Hollow.

In 1956, even though he was weakened by a
major heart attack suffered the previous year,
Jesse, along with Naomi, returned to education at
a financial loss to themselves. Jesse again accepted the principalship of McKell High School and
Naomi taught in the elementary grades. Because of
his health, Stuart could not continue in that
position longer than one year.

Since the late 1950's Stuart has periodically
accepted a number of the teaching positions for
which he is in constant demand all over the United
States. In the summer of 1958 Stuart taught courses
in the graduate college of education and in creative
writing at the University of Nevada. In 1960 Jesse,
Naomi, and daughter Jane Stuart traveled to Cairo,
Egypt, where Jesse accepted a position as a Visiting
Professor at the American University. Mrs. Stuart
taught in the American Elementary and Secondary
School and Jane completed her freshman year at the
University of Cairo.

In 1962 Stuart was sponsored by the United
States State Department in a lecture tour around
the world. Accompanied by Mrs. Stuart, the educator
from W-Hollow lectured to audiences in Iran, Korea,
Egypt, Greece, Lebanon, West Pakistan, East Pakistan,
the Phillippines, and the Republic of Free China.[4]

During his lifetime, Stuart has served as a
guest lecturer at colleges and universities throughout the United States. He has addressed many state
assemblies of the N.E.A., and students from Harvard
to Lincoln Memorial have had the rare privilege of
hearing a living embodiment of Frost's "old truths

117

we keep coming back to" as Stuart the educator has
consistently proclaimed the message that the basis
of American democracy must be an educated people
and that an educated man is a majority of one who
can make a difference not only in his own life but
in the life of his country.

Stuart wrote the first of his four autobio-
graphical-educational novels as a result of a term
paper assignment by Dr. Mims of Vanderbilt University.[5] Beyond Dark Hills is one of the greatest
American autobiographical novels ever written.
Throughout its pages Stuart recounts the struggle
of the Appalachian people for self-sufficiency
from the days of virgin land and timber to his own
desperate fight to obtain an education. The narrator chooses a path beyond the encircling confines
of his dark hills to Plum Grove School, Greenup
High School, Lincoln Memorial and Vanderbilt
Universities. In perhaps the greatest educational
odyssey in the history of American literature,
the narrator returns to the dark hills of home,
but he returns on his own terms as an educated man:

> His book gives you the picture in all its
> detail, all aspects of the hill community's
> life from birth to death, the sights and
> sounds of all the seasons, the range and
> variety in human nature that the smallest
> place can show to one who knows it well
> and sees it clearly. And it gives you the
> story of Jesse Stuart's emergence from
> that background. . . . Many an American
> education has been worked and fought for
> as hard as Jesse Stuart worked and fought
> for his, but I don't know where that
> story has been told with such convincing
> effect as Jesse Stuart has told it here.
> Beyond Dark Hills is, in its implications,
> more than a personal record; it is a
> chapter in the American story.[6]

The second of Stuart's educational-autobio-
graphical novels, The Thread That Runs So True,
was first published in 1949. The events described
in this novel took place from 1923-1939, and Stuart

118

has stated that his intention was not to write a literary novel but rather "to wake a sleeping public up to the value of educating their youth and greatness of the dedicated teacher."[7]

The heroic dedication of the teacher-narrator of The Thread That Runs So True is a tribute to many American secondary and elementary teachers, particularly in the Appalachian school system-- great Americans who have received so few dollars to educate the nation's youth. Readers of Thread cannot refrain from admiring the narrator as he teaches fifty-four classes, at age seventeen, to the pupils of the one-room Lonesome Valley School and shows them the practical value of education; as he returns from college and becomes principal and the faculty to the fourteen brilliant students of Winston High and walks seventeen miles through winter snow to obtain library books for them; and as he returns from graduate school to become Superintendent of Greenwood County Schools and fight for the educational good of all teachers and students against a typically corrupt and myopic Appalachian Board of Education.

Thread is no fairy tale and the narrator wages a heroic battle for education during these desperate years for both American and Appalachian education:

> Thus, in the fateful years between 1912 and 1927 which so strongly influenced the whole future of the coalfield, that which it needed was aborted and lost. Its foremost need was for a comprehensive and effective system of public education to gather up this rich human material from a dozen states and many countries and convert it into a wise and virtuous citizenry. But this foremost requirement was denied it. The schools were robbed of adequate financing. The best teachers, those with the richest gifts of inspiration and experience, drifted away, and a vicious system of intellectual inbreeding was established which has never been broken.[8]

119

As have countless Appalachian educators, the
narrator of Thread leaves his beloved mother of
professions because he cannot earn a decent living
even as principal of a large county high school.
The story of his inspirational teaching and his
fight for quality education is truly an American
epic: "The Thread That Runs So True is dedicated
to The Teachers of America but it is every American's book, as indigenously epic as the Paul
Bunyan saga and with a hero possessed of brains
as well as brawn."[9]

Jesse Stuart has always been committed to the
value of the free public school system and the
vital role it plays as the cornerstone of American
democracy. The depth of that commitment was firmly
illustrated in 1956 as Stuart was permitted by his
doctor to assume the principalship of McKell High
School while convalescing from a major heart attack
of the previous year. Stuart had heard disturbing
talk regarding the condition of McKell High School,
the beloved school he had directed to such heights
twenty years previously, and he decided the school
needed him. Jesse and Naomi Stuart taught at
McKell for one year at a financial loss--their
salaries placing them in a higher tax bracket.
Mr. Gallion's School is the story of that year,
and this novel has some special things to say to
educators, parents, school board members, people
who financially exploit students, and taxpayers.[10]

The narrator, Professor George Gallion, maintains that the fault of the children is that they
have too much security--economic, social, and
psychological; he feels that too much money and
soft living have caused this problem. The blame
for poor schools in Appalachia he sees as the
people's: half do not care and the other half
want something for nothing. Gallion is disgusted
by the resultant moral disintegration at Kensington High (McKell High School in real life), and
he maintains that corruption in young people is
caused by corruption in parents, churches, and
the law.[11]

By the end of the year, George Gallion has
solved most of Kensington High's problems and

turned her youth in the right direction. Windows are intact, the grounds are attractive, academics are taken seriously, and the students have pride in their school. George Gallion has accomplished this modern miracle in education through the unrelenting application of one a priori rule to himself, to parents, to the faculty and to the student body --"The Buck Stops Here!" Mr. Gallion's School is not only a great Appalachian novel but a great American novel:

> For here is a . . . believable American high school in trouble, and it is treated through the complex vision of a mature persona at once active and enigmatic, egotistical and kind, unorthodox and imaginative, comic and grave, wise and not infrequently--powerful.
> By the end of the novel, Gallion's school has become a citadel of learning, high on a hill "in a world of darkness, bathed in light," emblematic of the human spirit caught in the eternal conflict between good and evil. Gallion is a committed man in an uncommitted world, and he makes the reader believe that one man can make a difference.[12]

Contrary to the popular stereotype of the dominant culture, Jesse Stuart has persistently maintained that education is far from impossible in the Appalachian subculture: "You know I just attended a program called 'The Paradox of Learning in Appalachia,' and I stood up and said there wasn't any paradox. The brightest and most rewarding minds I've ever worked with have been right here in these hills."[13]

To Teach, To Love is Stuart's tribute to the outstanding teachers and students the author has known in his fifty-year involvement with education. From reading the novel, one comes to the understanding that Jesse Stuart is indisputably one of America's most prominent educators and writers about education--a teacher and administrator who was perfecting many innovative practices in the

education of Appalachians long before such inno-
vations became popular in the greater American
educational system.

In the preface of To Teach, To Love Stuart
maintains that he never thought of his prospective
pupils as deprived and that he has always believed
in education for the masses: "We never called our
kids from the Kentucky hills 'culturally deprived,'
though many of their folks couldn't read or write;
we just taught them and they learned. . . . In the
public schools where I have worked--where all may
enter and not be selected for any particular
reason--I learned to agree with Thomas Jefferson.
I, too, have faith in the masses."[14]

The computerizing and depersonalizing of so
much of the modern educational process is foreign
to the narrator of this novel, who assumes the
textbook as only a starting point for teacher and
student and who makes the educational process
vitally meaningful in the local frame of reference:

> All members of the class agree at the
> first of the year to write about the
> things in our own backyards. We would
> write about anything and everything ex-
> cept picnics (that was a subject worn
> out long ago) and trips to New York,
> unless the student had actually been
> there. We decided to write about our
> own people, our trees, stars, grass,
> flowers--old apple orchards in the sun
> and tumbling fences, people getting
> drunk, elections, public officials,
> love affairs that the students actually
> know of . . . , snakes, turtles, ter-
> rapins, birds--all living things that
> walk or crawl on earth." (209)

The dominant culture's belief in an ever increasing and impersonal technology as the solution
to the problems of American education is anathema
to the Appalachian ethos of the narrator of To
Teach, To Love, and he maintains that such an
attitude is wreaking havoc among the youth of
America:

So what has happened to our people in America? Why do we have almost fifty percent dropouts before our young people reach the twelfth grade? It cannot be denied in America that our main motive in education is to "make life easier." We have tried to replace all labor with machines, even machines to think for us. We have even tried to invent a teaching machine to replace the teacher. We have mechanical slaves to do ninety percent of our work. No wonder our youth drop out of school! What is there for them out there in our bleak future? Why become a number, a zip code, a cipher? (304-305)

Jesse Stuart finds it regrettable that a teacher cannot give A pluses where the computer doesn't make pluses,[15] and he would rather have a pupil who makes C grades and has A character than one who makes A grades and has C character; it is Stuart's belief that the morals and character of our country rest upon the morals and character of the people.[16] For this reason the narrator-educator of To Teach, To Love has difficulty understanding how America can underestimate the worth of its schools and he is not proud of the way his native country has treated its teachers (205).

Several times during his lifetime Stuart has had more than enough of the inadequate wages paid to teachers, and he has quit education many times, vowing never to return; but he has kept returning to his beloved profession because of two factors— his great love for youth and his desire to help them learn. Stuart is truly afflicted with the malady of all great educators everywhere—a terminal deposit of chalk dust in the veins: "What is it about September with teachers and school people, when the leaves turn color and you see the children going down the dusty road to the little school, walking down the leaf-strewn city streets to the high school? You see the football in the air, and the young teacher uneasy in the schoolyard, and the new boy being sized up, and

the books under the arms . . . something gets
under our skins" (66).

For many millions of people in Stuart's Appalachian subculture, education is the only way to
break out of a deadly slough of hopelessness:
"A small fraction of the money now dispensed in
relief checks would build attractive schoolhouses,
fill them with books and laboratories, and educate
competent teachers for their faculties. Until such
schools are provided--for so long as the present
drab facilities are symbolic of learning, inspiration and hope--there will be no real alternative
to the dry rot of Welfarism."[17]

Throughout Stuart's lifetime work in education,
there runs one overriding theme--his commitment to
the youth of America. When a concerned mother once
complained to Stuart about the lack of reading by
"our sons" and asked how to remedy this deplorable
situation, Stuart replied: "Kick in the television
set--throw away the car keys."[18]

Education has played a great role in Stuart's
life and the lives of those around him. On May 6,
1959, the Louisville Downtown Optimist Club named
Jesse Stuart "Man of The Year" for the author's
"outstanding service to the youth of Kentucky."[19]
On November 9, 1966, Jefferson County's (Louisville,
Ky.) Jesse Stuart High School was dedicated. In
the late 1960's Stuart offered to sell forty-five
acres of his land as a proposed school site to the
Greenup County Board of Education for a price of
$1.00. Stuart, his brother and two sisters have
a combined total of twenty-seven years of college
education and over one hundred years of classroom
teaching; Stuart holds fifteen honorary doctoral
degrees from various American colleges and universities.[20] His wife, Naomi Deane, has a master's
degree in education and a life-time of teaching;
and his one child, Jessica Jane Jurgensmeyer,
holds a Ph.D. from Indiana University.

Stuart has waged a lifelong heroic battle
against the corruption of the Appalachian school
system, where every two years school board members
are elected and hire the county superintendent--

invariably one of the most powerful figures in the county.[21] In Kentucky a county school board member is required to have only an eighth grade education or the equivalent. The county board members and the superintendent hire and fire teachers, many of whom have graduate degrees.

When Stuart became the superintendent of Greenup County schools, he paid no attention to politics or politicians in running the schools and attacking the archaic trustee system. As a result he faced thirty-two lawsuits in one year and was hospitalized following a blackjack attack.[22] Undaunted, Stuart has continued to wage a lifetime war for the youth of Appalachia, America and the world.

Throughout a lifetime as one of America's most distinguished educators and writers on education, Stuart has consistently advocated Matthew Arnold's concept of learning as a process that leads to a knowledge of the best that has been thought and said in the world--a process that can and does lead to sweetness and light: "Books I have read, books I have recommended and taught youth in high school and college, have become a part of me. They will go with my mind, my flesh and body someday to a Plum Grove Grave. But the dream will escape. It will be there for others to see, to read, to dream and feel on the printed page, . . . and whatever I am, they have helped to shape and make me as they have helped to make and shape others through the centuries and millenniums."[23]

As early as 1949, in The Thread That Runs So True, Jesse Stuart stated: "If some writer could spring from the teaching profession and do a great book to honor his profession, he would be immortal. For no other profession in America has directly or indirectly influenced the destiny of so many people as the teaching profession" (202). That writer is Jesse Stuart, and he produced not one, but four great books: Beyond Dark Hills, The Thread That Runs So True, Mr. Gallion's School, and To Teach, To Love. In 1970 Stuart stated:

125

"As a teacher, I have tried to go beyond the
textbooks into the character--stressing honesty,
goodness, and making each life count for something.
I have written thirty-two books, nearly four
hundred short stories, two hundred articles and
essays, and two thousand poems, trying to share
my dream. I have tried to arouse and awaken our
people through more than five thousand lectures.
I shall do more."[24]

No other author in the history of American
letters can stand by Stuart in Stuart's portrayal
of our educational system from elementary school
to graduate study, that ever-expanding epic journey of the mind:

It is most painful now as I
Schoolmaster once return to this;
Master of learning, all they had
Until they grew and went beyond.
This barn was dear to them and me,
Only the skeleton remains;
Parts of the roof, windows and doors
And master's desk and window panes
Have gone into oblivion.

The birds and bats now carry on
Where elm trees have reached new heights;
Young winds blow over greened-up fields
That lie in all directions here.
Legions of grass run with the winds,
Yet winds and grass have not erased
The memories of what has been
From those who caught fire here that spread
The flame of learning to the world.[25]

NOTES

1. T. N. Bethel, Pat Gish and Tom Gish, "Kennedy Hears of Need," in <u>Appalachia in the Sixties</u>, ed. by David S. Walls and John B. Stephenson (Lexington, Ky.: University Press of Kentucky, 1972), p. 68.

2. Jesse Stuart, "Poverty of the Mind," <u>Kappa Delta Pi Record</u>, 6 (Dec. 1969), 56.

3. Betty Garrett, "An Appalachian Author Describes His Life Style," <u>Appalachia</u>, 6 (Dec. 1972-Jan. 1973), 25.

4. John Gilpin, <u>The Man...Jesse Stuart</u> (Ashland, Ky.: Economy Printers, 1968), pp. 1-13.

5. Jesse Stuart, untitled MS, Murray State University Library, pp. 21-22. /Note: All manuscript references are to the massive Stuart collection at Murray State University, Murray, Kentucky./

6. J. Donald Adams, "Jesse Stuart's Homespun Story," review of <u>Beyond Dark Hills</u>, by Jesse Stuart, in the <u>New York Times Book Review</u>, April 24, 1971, pp. 24-25.

7. "Jesse Stuart's Characters in the Flesh," Louisville (Ky.) <u>Courier-Journal</u> Magazine section, 27 Oct., 1963, p. 30.

8. Harry M. Caudill, <u>Night Comes to the Cumberlands</u> (Boston: Little, Brown, 1962), pp. 136-137.

9. Worth Tuttle Hedden, "When Jesse Stuart Fought and Taught," review of <u>The Thread That Runs So True</u>, by Jesse Stuart, in the <u>New York Herald Tribune Book Review</u>, Sept. 25, 1949, p. 24.

10. Mary Leonhard, "Kentucky Hill Folk Change," review of <u>Mr. Gallion's School</u>, by Jesse Stuart, in the <u>Arizona Republic</u>, Nov. 12, 1967, p. 9.

127

11. Jesse Stuart, Mr. Gallion's School (New York: McGraw Hill, 1967), p. 262.

12. H. Edward Richardson, "Reviews of 'Mr. Gallion's School'," review of Mr. Gallion's School, by Jesse Stuart, in the Los Angeles Examiner, July 28, 1968, p. 13.

13. Betty Garrett, "An Appalachian Author Describes His Life Style," 27.

14. Jesse Stuart, To Teach, To Love (New York: The World Publishing Company, 1970), pp. 7,9.

15. Betty Garrett, "An Appalachian Author Describes His Life Style," 28.

16. Stuart, To Teach, To Love, p. 187.

17. Caudill, Night Comes to the Cumberlands, p. 288.

18. "Kick in TV, throw away car keys, Author Recommends," Ashland (Ky.) Daily Independent, 21 Nov. 1957, p. 6.

19. Louisville (Ky.) Courier-Journal, 6 May 1959, p. 6.

20. Jesse Stuart, "A Gift For Learning and Light," Greenup (Ky.) News, 28 Jan. 1971, p. 1.

21. Caudill, Night Comes to the Cumberlands, p. 336.

22. Stuart, To Teach, To Love, pp. 71, 172.

23. Jesse Stuart, "The Importance of Reading in the Life of Man," Kappa Delta Pi Record, 5 (Oct, 1968), 14.

24. Stuart, To Teach, To Love, p. 308.

25. Jesse Stuart, untitled poem, Saturday Evening Post, 232:81 (July 25, 1959).

128

CHAPTER EIGHT

JESSE STUART--AMERICAN POET

"Sedge and Muddy Waters"

In his poetry Jesse Stuart is Mr. Appalachia
just as Robert Frost is Mr. New England--both are
major American poets who happen to base their work
on a specific region of the country. Stuart is
undeniably a major poet by reason of his produc-
tiveness and skill, but there has long been an
undeserved tentativeness among some critics in the
recognition given his work. Even his friendliest
critics have sold him somewhat short because of
the old myth of Stuart as a regionalist plowboy.
Stuart has plowed, but he is hardly a plowboy.
It is time that criticism begin to take full account not only of his fruitfulness (over 2,000
poems) and his popularity but also of the wide
experience of the world and the sound scholarship
that underlies his work.

Stuart's first book of poetry, Harvest of
Youth, was published privately in 1930. It is a
collection of poems written while Stuart was a
high school and college student and set some of
the themes he was to return to in later work.
But Harvest of Youth was only the beginning of a
remarkable poetic career, one that is still continuing as this is written. Throughout this career
Stuart has grown in wisdom and skill, becoming a
poet of unqualified greatness.

With the publication of Man With A Bull-Tongue
Plow (a collection of 703 sonnets) in 1934, Jesse
Stuart achieved instant fame. But, as has been
typical with Stuart's work, the reviews were mixed.
When Mark Van Doren, for example, praised Stuart
as "an American Burns," Louis Untermeyer resented
the comparison, maintaining that Stuart's lyricism
had none of the careful planning characteristic of
Burns.[1] There are some signs in his article that
Untermeyer was simply overwhelmed by the bulk of

Stuart's book.[2] Two 1938 articles in _Time_ magazine
show the same division of opinion. In one of them
Stuart is patronizingly referred to as "a six-foot,
207-lb., 30-year-old Kentucky hillbilly."[3] In the
other the same man is called "one of the most
promising U.S. poets."[4]

Untermeyer's criticism, the "hillbilly re-
mark, and a host of other comments on Stuart's
supposed crudeness are typical of a demonstrably
unfair but remarkably persistent theme in Stuart
criticism--Stuart is not to be taken seriously as
a poet because he represents an inferior culture
and because he is personally unlearned. The high,
or low, point in this critical tradition was
reached when John Gould Fletcher, writing in
Poetry magazine, rejected the Burns comparison.
Stuart is nothing like Burns, Fletcher maintained,
because Burns had behind him "a wealth of folk
song, old minstrelsy, and rough ballad-making,"
whereas the Kentucky poet wrote from no tradition
at all and, besides, knew nothing of the poet's
craft.[5] Fletcher's appraisal shows an almost
complete ignorance about Appalachia and about his
subject's life. It would be nice to dismiss it
out of hand, except that the attitude Fletcher
spoke for is still alive and still keeping Jesse
Stuart from taking the place he deserves and has
worked hard for among major American poets.

Granted that influential critics like
Fletcher knew little of Appalachia in the 1930's,
Jesse Stuart's long and excellent apprenticeship
as a poet should not have been overlooked, even
then, in considering his work. The high level of
achievement reached in the sonnets of _Man With A
Bull-Tongue Plow_ did not materialize from a vacuum:
Stuart had been painstakingly learning his craft
for several years both from the wealth of Appalachian balladry and from a series of more conventional sources.

During his high school career, Stuart had
read all of the library books in Greenup High:
Emerson, Thoreau, Hawthorne, and de Maupassant
were among his favorite authors.[6] Mrs. Robert
Hatton, his excellent and demanding high school

English teacher was a graduate of the University
of Missouri School of Journalism. Stuart has said
that he felt "a power from on high" sent this great
teacher to him as at this early date she taught
creative writing one day a week to her English
classes.[7] Mrs. Hatton introduced him to Robert
Burns--whose poetry literally set Stuart afire
with the urge to write. Working in the Armco
Steel Mill in Ashland, Kentucky, as a young man
saving for a college education, Stuart bought a
book a week and was reading nightly such authors
as Robert Frost, Edgar Lee Masters, Edna Millay,
Malcom Cowley, Rupert Brooke, Amy Lowell, Edwin
Markham and others. At this time, Carl Sandburg
was his favorite poet.[8]

At Lincoln Memorial and Vanderbilt universities Stuart encountered a series of excellent
teachers who contributed further to shaping his
natural genius. At Lincoln Memorial, Stuart was
a wildly enthusiastic student of Harry Harrison
Kroll, a publishing southern novelist who demanded
30,000 words per quarter from his students.[9] As
a graduate student at Vanderbilt University, a
place that Stuart referred to as "an English
heaven," Stuart's teacher of destiny was Donald
Davidson:

> But the one class where I rejoiced was
> in Donald Davidson's Elizabethan Poetry.
> Donald Davidson was the only one of my
> Vanderbilt Professors who said: "Stuart,
> you are an A student." And when I showed
> him the two kinds of poems I had written,
> one about my country and the people,
> which was natural to me and the other one
> where I was trying to write in the popu-
> lar vogue of the day, like T. S. Eliot,
> Ezra Pound, John Donne, and Carl Sandburg,
> he told me to write about what was natural
> to me and in the way I could write best.
> He chose my natural poems over the others,
> revised one and told me to send it to the
> American Mercury where Henry Mencken was
> editor. . . . "You don't belong to the
> little magazines," he said. "You belong
> to the big ones." I could hardly believe

this. "Go home and write of your country like the Irish write of their country, in fact you're a lot like the Irish."[10]

Upon Stuart's departure from Vanderbilt, Donald Davidson clasped his hand and told him he hoped someday Jesse would have a million readers.[11]

It was against this background of hard study and preparation that Stuart wrote 703 poems and called them Man With A Bull-Tongue Plow. In 1946 this volume of poetry was selected as one of the best 100 books in America and one of the 1000 great books of the world.[12] Nor is it at all true, as some of his critics have thought, that Jesse Stuart has no perspective beyond his home hill country. In April of 1937, as a result of this collection, Stuart was awarded a Guggenheim fellowship, and his project was "to study the likenesses in literature and folklore between the Scotish highlanders and their American counterparts, as well as the similarities in personality and mode of life." Stuart visited England, Scotland, and most of the countries of Europe. He was especially impressed by the Scotch Highlanders: "Physically they seem the hardest and strongest. They live frugally and make the best soldiers Great Britain has. And the Mountain People of Kentucky are the same."[13]

While in London, Stuart accepted Lady Astor's repeated invitation for him to visit her. Stuart decided to accept and visit his distant kin: Lady Astor was a Langley from Virginia who was related to the Stuarts of Virginia. Stuart had a two-week visit with Lord and Lady Astor, and he attended the House of Commons with Lady Astor. During his stay at the Astor estate, he spent some evenings in London with struggling British, Irish and Welsh poets, who would accompany him home in order to watch him enter the grounds.[14]

Stuart has said that in the years which have followed Man With A Bull-Tongue Plow that, regardless of whatever else he has done, he has continued to write poems: poems that "came like April

showers."[15] He got his idea for his third book
of poems while looking through an old family album.
Album of Destiny, consisting of 444 poems, and
first published in 1944, was eleven years in the
writing. Stuart has maintained that he spent more
time and effort on Album of Destiny than on any
other of his books.[16] He poured into it the resources of what was already an exceptionally rich
life and education, and this time the reviewers
began to see what Jesse Stuart was about. One
critic, writing in the New York Times, praised
the high level of skill of Album's poet: "Except
for Conrad Aiken, nobody among living American
poets commands the beauty of the single line with
more power than Jesse Stuart. . . . Album of Destiny is his best and places him in the first rank.
Granted that he needs more self-criticism, that
his collections need winnowing, that his essential
folk quality is only at its best when he adds to
it the refinement of which he is capable, he remains, in a generous proportion of his work, one
of our greatest."[17]

In his review of Album in the Times of Los
Angeles, John Russell McCarthy accurately appraised
a vitally important facet of Stuart's poetic stance:
the fact that Jesse Stuart's intended audience is
the American people rather than any particular
clique:

> Jesse Stuart is one of those who are
> helping to bring American poetry back to
> American people. It is odd that such a
> task should be put on the shoulders of
> any poet, or any group of poets. But the
> truth remains that many of the poets who
> have been eagerly published and eagerly
> acclaimed by critics in the past twenty
> years have been poets who (1), were writ-
> ing only for their own pleasure and that
> of a small group who called themselves
> intelligentsia; (2) were writing for the
> followers of Mr. Frank Sinatra, Mr. Edgar
> Guest, and Mr. Harold Bell Wright.
> Jesse Stuart (thanks be!) ignores the
> odd top and the sad bottom: Jesse Stuart
> writes for the real American. He wrote

thus in "Man With A Bull-Tongue Plow."
He is again writing for the real American in "Album of Destiny."[18]

In 1952 Stuart published Kentucky Is My Land,
a moving and powerful poetic tribute to a state
and the character of its people, and in 1954 he
was made poet laureate of Kentucky. October 15,
1955, was proclaimed Jesse Stuart Day by the governor of Kentucky and was especially celebrated
in Greenup, Kentucky.

During the summer of 1959 Stuart appeared with
Robert Frost on a program at the Bread Loaf School
of English in Middlebury, Vermont, and spoke of a
discussion he had had on another occasion with his
fellow "Regionalist":

> Then, I went to the home of Robert
> Frost with Donald Davidson, my teacher
> at Vanderbilt University. Here, I got
> to see his woods, his roads, and home.
> He had high wires stretched around his
> garden to keep the deer from eating
> his vegetables. Looking in all direc-
> tions from his home, his country was
> beautiful.
> The first question Robert Frost
> asked me was what I thought of schools
> of poetry. I was slow to tell him what
> I actually thought. But he wasn't very
> slow about telling me what he thought.
> He disagreed with all of them. And
> when he discussed a school of poetry,
> he laughed loudly. He laughed at why
> a group of men's minds should unite in
> a school of art. He thought every poet
> should be an individualist. He explained
> this by saying if there was a grove of
> oaks growing in the forest, each would
> reach approximately the same size. If
> only one grew there, an individual oak,
> it might be a giant. It would be larger
> than any one of the grove. Then, he
> laughed again. I cannot forget his opin-
> ion of schools of poetry.[19]

Despite his many successes, however, Stuart's career seemed to have reached its lowest ebb in the late 1950's. During this decade many of the magazines that had published Stuart's work no longer existed, many of the editors who had accepted his poems were dead, and he was able to place only a trickle of work in print. He could find no publisher interested in a new collection of his poems, even though his three volumes had sold much better than the average for poetry, and he felt certain that he would never again have a book of poems published. He was ready to accept the fact that he would never again achieve wide acceptance as a poet.

It was in this frame of mind that, in 1960, Stuart accepted a position as visiting professor in English and Education at the American University in Cairo, Egypt. And then, on February 2, 1961, he suddenly learned he had been awarded the 1960 $5,000 Fellowship of the Academy of American Poets by a majority vote of twelve chancellors: J. Donald Adams, W. H. Auden, Witter Bynner, H. S. Canby, Max Eastman, Robert Hillyer, Randall Jarrell, Marianne Moore, Robert Nathan, John G. Niehardt, Frederick A. Pottle, and John H. Wheelock:

> Always before when I received some honor, I had rejoiced. Now, when I read the well known names on this list of authors, scholars, editors, and one publisher, names familiar to millions of Americans and among them better-known authors than I, I wept. The caliber of the men and women who had voted this award to me was a greater honor than the financial renumeration. This made up for all the losses, heartaches, and rejections I had received with poetry from my high school days to the present.[20]

But the rejection of Stuart's work was still not over. The American Poets award opened the way to publication of Hold April, which appeared in 1962 to typically mixed reviews. Robert Hillyer, a Pulitzer Prize poet, maintained that Hold April

135

was "A beautiful book . . . with its own golden place in our too-often shadowy literature." But another critic was offended by the poems and accused them of "hiding scars with loveliness,"[21] overlooking the book's focus on Stuart's beloved mountain spring season and reacting as if Appalachia's most sensitive spokesman and staunchest advocate was suddenly trying to sugar-coat the problems he had spent his life fighting. Stuart has not been notably lucky in his critics.

Writing is a very personal matter, perhaps expecially so for Jesse Stuart, who writes by conviction from experience. Harsh criticism has withered many an author's independence. But there is no evidence that adverse reviews have ever affected Stuart's writing.

At the very beginning of his career as a poet, Stuart wisely heeded the advice of H. L. Mencken and Robert Frost, who told him not to answer critics who were attacking his style of poetry.[22] One major criticism levelled at Stuart is the modernist charge that the sonnet form is no longer permissible in the twentieth century. When Jesse Stuart and Carl Sandburg, another of his poet friends, were speaking at a war-bond drive in Chicago in the late winter of 1943, Sandburg asked why Stuart ever started writing in "that damned restricted form?" Stuart's answer is typical of his attitude toward the critics: "Because a man visiting Vanderbilt University when I was a student there told me not to use it."[23]

Stuart has proclaimed that writing poems is almost as essential to him as breathing or eating. He has further stated that whether his way of creating poems is the right way or not, it is right for him; Stuart feels, as did Robert Frost, that it would be impossible for him to belong to a school of poetry unless it would be built around or over him: his poetry has to be written his way. He has said that he does not expect or even wish other poets to agree with him but grants them the freedom to write any way they wish or any way they can.[22] Stuart believes that "time, and time alone, is an author's greatest critic."[25]

On the two-hundredth anniversary of Robert
Burns' birth, Stuart was invited by Centre College,
Danville, Kentucky, to give a lecture on Scotland's
great poet. "The Burns Lecture" provides vital
insight into Stuart's beliefs regarding schools
of poetry and to the unfair treatment that subculture poets have traditionally received at the hands
of dominant culture critics. Jesse Stuart, the
greatest poet the Appalachian culture has yet produced, has often received from American critics
the same type of culturally prejudiced consideration
that Robert Burns of Scotland received at the hands
of many English reviewers.

In "The Burns Lecture" Stuart maintained that
although Robert Burns's father was a poor tenant
farmer and Burns was doing a man's job of farm
work at the age of fifteen, the old idea that the
poet was an ignorant farm boy will have to be
abandoned. Stuart further pointed out that at
Burns' untimely death, which was a shock to all of
Scotland, people were awakened to the fact that he
was a genius "who would make their country and its
people live as long as time lasted." Stuart then
told his audience that Robert Burns, a poet who
covered the complete range of human emotions, is
now more widely read throughout the world than any
other poet except Shakespeare--another "native
genius."

In this lecture Stuart asked how Burns would
be received if he were to appear in contemporary
America, where poets swim in schools, control
publication, award prizes, and leave "nonunion"
writers on the outside looking in--with the result
that poetry is hardly printed because people will
not buy it: "Behind our false veneering is much
of the hypocrisy and sham which Robert Burns encountered in Scotland in his day. Writers in
England at that time had set the fashions for
would-be young literary lions to follow. Robert
Burns' fresh, natural, human-heart poetry, which
reflected the joys, sorrows, struggles of his time
and of his people, burst these literary concepts
like shot from a shotgun puncturing airborn bal-
loons. He didn't have to attack them. They had

to attack him. His two books took poetry away from the cultists and gave it back young and alive to the people."[26]

All his life Stuart has followed Burns's program, fighting tenaciously for his right to make poetry his way and about his own people. During his first year at Lincoln Memorial, Stuart took one of his hill sonnets to Miss Kathryn Howard--who did not allow her students to read Burns. Miss Howard took equally strong exception to Stuart's work: "I don't like your sonnet at all. Get away from sedge and muddy waters and the night wind. Write of high beautiful things like Shakespeare, Keats, Browning, and Longfellow. Don't waste your time on low vile things."[27] It is precisely Jesse Stuart's glory as a poet that he has never knuckled under to such pressure.

Following his meeting with his beloved Robert Frost at Breadloaf College in 1959, Stuart traveled in all of the New England states and found Frost everywhere: "He was Mr. New England. He had portrayed his country in original, philosophical, and character poems. His words and lines were of great character, strength, and power. They were chiseled from New England granite. Robert Frost didn't have a bag of critical tools to rule others out and himself in. He didn't need to have these. He was already inside where he was a permanent world fixture."[28]

Jesse Stuart is Mr. Appalachia in the same way, indisputably one of the greatest masters of the sonnet form in English and American poetry. His fourteen, fifteen, and sixteen line sonnets capture universal truths though they are deeply tied to his land and people. They are written for all men.

In his effort to be true to his unchanging goal--to write honestly and to write for all men--Stuart himself has changed. His later works are a far cry from the early poems in Harvest of Youth. The themes are still the great timeless truths of existence that have occupied him through a lifetime of poetry, but recent Stuart poems reflect some

138

surprising influences. For example, Stuart's
"The Crow's Dark Night," published during the
winter of 1967, contains many clear echoes of
the modern British poet Ted Hughes:

This is the day the hungry mouse runs out
To find a grain of corn and there's not any . . .
Looks like the mouse could see snow lies about
In drifting heaps around the logshack shanty.
The crows sail over in the treacherous skies
And fight against the currents of the wind;
I watch their struggling hard and hear their cries
Above white land where grain is hard to find.
Crows fly and call, their craws are empty now
And little brown woodmouse is hungry too
Since winter's scanty food is under snow,
Woodmouse and crows can't have a rendezvous,
Mouse-morsel to whet one crow's appetite;
Woodmouse had better stay in his cozy log
Than be a part of hungry crow's dark night.[29]

Such modern plainness may seem surprising
to those who do not know Stuart well, but it is
typical of the way he has always brought the sum
of his constantly growing experience to his work,
producing poetry of increasing ripeness and matu-
rity. If Stuart's belief that time is the ultimate critic and the proper determiner of poets is
correct, he has gone about his career in the way
calculated to win the ultimate rave review. Long
after time has wasted the current generation,
many of Jesse Stuart's poems will still be here--
friends to man:

Oh dear Lum Dryasdust! You are taking
poetry along with you. It doesn't have
you by the heels and drag you everywhere
you go, through the steel mills, through
the pasture fields and the cornfields,
through the tie-timber woods, at the plow,
and everywhere you go. No, you are going
to sit down and write poetry when you get
ready. All I have to say is, don't tell
everybody about it. Poetry puts you down
and makes you write. Edgar Allan Poe is
not going to tell you to do anything.
You have to be your own self.[30]

NOTES

1. Louis Untermeyer, "Six Poets," review of
   Man With A Bull-Tongue Plow by Jesse Stuart,
   and five other books of poetry, in American
   Mercury, April 1935, pp. 506-507.

2. Ibid.

3. "Uninhibited Poet," review of Beyond Dark
   Hills, by Jesse Stuart, in Time, April 18,
   1938, p. 77.

4. "Greenup Poet," Time, 7 Nov. 1938, p. 62.

5. John Gould Fletcher, "Kentucky Georgics,"
   review of Man With A Bull-Tongue Plow, by
   Jesse Stuart, in Poetry, Jan. 1935, pp. 217-
   220.

6. Frank Hartwell Leavell, The Literary Career
   of Jesse Stuart (Ann Arbor, Michigan: University Microfilms, Inc., 1965), p. 28.

7. Jesse Stuart, "Writing's Been Good to Me,"
   Writer's Digest, Nov. 1977, p. 20.

8. Leavell, Literary Career, pp. 36-37.

9. Stuart, "Writing's Been Good to Me," p. 21.

10. Jesse Stuart, untitled MS, Murray State Uni-
    versity Library, p. 21. ⟦Note: All manuscript
    references are to the massive Stuart collection
    at Murray State University, Murray, Kentucky.⟧

11. Jesse Stuart, To Teach, To Love (New York:
    The World Publishing Company, 1970), p. 163.

12. Ish Richey, Kentucky Literature (Tompkinsville,
    Kentucky: Monroe County Press, 1963), p. 163.

13. Leavell, Literary Career, pp. 89, 90.

14. Stuart, To Teach, To Love, pp. 205, 206.

15. Jesse Stuart, _A Jesse Stuart Reader_ (New York: McGraw Hill, 1963), p. 293.

16. Ibid.

17. "Among the New Volumes of Verse," review of _Album of Destiny_, by Jesse Stuart, in New York _Times_, Dec. 10, 1944, Sec. 7, p. 29.

18. John Russell McCarthy, "Jesse Stuart's Poetry," review of _Album of Destiny_, by Jesse Stuart, in Los Angeles _Times_, Dec. 16, 1944.

19. Jesse Stuart, "Meeting Mr. New England, America's Greatest Poet," MS. 69-1 M-1, pp. 1-2, Murray Kentucky University Library.

20. Stuart, _Stuart Reader_, pp. 293, 294, 295.

21. Webster Schott, "Should Poetry Hide Scars?" review of _Hold April_, by Jesse Stuart, in Kansas City _Star_, May 19, 1962.

22. Dick Perry, _Reflections of Jesse Stuart on a Land of Many Moods_ (New York: McGraw Hill, 1971), p. 62.

23. Jesse Stuart, "Sandburg, My Hero," _Lincoln Herald_, 70, No. 1 (Spring 1968), Lincoln Memorial University Press, 43.

24. Stuart, _Stuart Reader_, p. 292.

25. Jesse Stuart, "Autobiographical Reminiscence," University of _Kansas City Review_, XXCII, No. 1 (Oct. 1960), p. 58.

26. Jesse Stuart, "The Burns Lecture," _Peabody Reflector_, XL, No. 5 (Sept.-Oct. 1967), pp. 237-239.

27. Stuart, _To Teach, To Love_, p. 110.

28. Stuart, "Meeting Mr. New England," p. 3.

29. Jesse Stuart, "The Crow's Dark Night," _Southwest Review_, LII, No. 1 (Winter 1967), p. 12.

30. Stuart, <u>To Teach, To Love</u>, p. 143.

Stuart at home with friends.
Home later remodeled in 1948.

CHAPTER NINE

JESSE STUART--AMERICAN SHORT STORY WRITER

"That Stark and Beautiful Land"

In considering Jesse Stuart's achievement and reputation as a short story writer, a person is almost overwhelmed by numbers--the number of his stories, the number of times they have been reprinted and translated, the number of awards he has won, the number of favorable reviews, and, lately, the number of times his claims to be considered a great master of the form have been slighted or rejected.

Stuart was blessed with a tremendous relish for writing, and he has needed every bit of it. As a young boy with prodigious natural talent, he was fascinated with the magic of words. As a high school student, he showed an altogether untypical love of theme writing, sometimes volunteering as many as twelve themes on an assignment and reading them to the great entertainment of the class. But his gift was not always appreciated. As a young college student he was told by many of his teachers and an even greater number of publishers that he could not write short stories or novels.[1] Stuart maintains it was three teachers-- Mrs. R. E. Hatton of Greenup High School, Harry Harrison Kroll of Lincoln Memorial, and Donald Davidson of Vanderbilt--and the inspiration of one book that kept his dedication alive: "I've read so many of the world's great books but not one has been as influential as that dust covered one placed on the floor with door ajar so I could see in the Greenup High School janitorial room, Guy de Maupassant's The Odd Number. Three teachers and a book have been the great influences to send my books to libraries, schools, and homes over America and to countries and peoples on six of the Earth's Continents."[2]

But this is only part of the story--as has
been true of many of the world's great authors,
Stuart has his own literary demon to make him go.
He has said that his short stories are born from
mental impressions, including characters and scenes
so vivid he is compelled to write them down: "I
cannot anymore keep from creating stories than I
can stop breathing air into my lungs. I have to
breathe to live and I also have to write stories
or die." From the age of 16 to the age of 56,
Stuart published 302 short stories.[3]

Throughout this highly prolific career as a
short story writer, Stuart has received wide acclaim. For example many of his stories appeared
in Edward O'Brien's annual selections of the best
short stories published in Story magazine--The Best
Short Stories--which was published annually from
1937-1943.[4] And this was not the empty honor it
may seem in today's market of depressed demand of
original stories. In these anthologies, Stuart
was in the company of giants. The Best Short
Stories of 1939 included stories by Jesse Stuart,
Ernest Hemingway, William Faulkner, Erskine Caldwell, and F. Scott Fitzgerald.[5] In The Best Short
Stories of 1943 Stuart appeared with William Faulkner, William Saroyan, and Eudora Welty--a collection
of thirty stories by well-known artists who also
"appear nearly annually in both the O. Henry Prize
Stories and the Best Stories."[6] In 1965 a Stuart
short story was selected as one of "50 of the best"
short stories for Story Jubilee from the hundreds
of short stories published in Story magazine since
its inception in 1931. This volume contained
stories by such authors as Sherwood Anderson,
William Faulkner, Tennessee Williams, Erskine
Caldwell, Carson McCullers, Norman Mailer, William
Saroyan, J. D. Salinger and Truman Capote.[7]

Stuart met Edward O'Brien, the original editor
of The Best Short Stories, in England in 1937.
O'Brien told Stuart: "You're the most natural
short story writer I have ever met. You sleep and
breathe the short story and you think in terms of
short stories." O'Brien awarded Stuart the highest
number of triple-starred short stories ever given

a British or an American writer.[8]

The following titles of collections of Stuart short stories, complete with selected critical responses, will perhaps indicate Stuart's possibly unequalled record of publication in the history of the American short story:

Head o' W-Hollow - 1936
George Milburn in the New Republic:
"One thing seems obvious . . . no one was ever taught from scratch to write so well."[9]

Ralph Thompson in the New York Times:
"A lot of water will go over the dam before Kentucky, or any other state, develops another writer with the art that is this 28-year-old farmer-poet-school teacher's."[10]

Men of the Mountains - 1941
Milton Rugoff in the New York Herald-Tribune: "As authentic as a cornfield in August, as crude as a lean-jawed farmer sweating behind his plow, as fresh as a mountain stream, come Jesse Stuart's narratives of the Kentucky hill country. They are the product of a regionalism as clear and untainted as any we have."[11]

Tales from the Plum Grove Hills - 1946
Nash K. Burger in the New York Times:
"It is an inner hope and sturdiness as well as a rustic unawareness which carries his characters through."[12]

Clearing in the Sky and Other Stories - 1950
Coleman Rosenberger in the New York Herald-Tribune Book Review: "The good earth of Jesse Stuart's native hills still produces an excellent yield. These twenty-one stories of Kentucky are tart, full-flavored, immensely readable. Here in rich abundance are Stuart's improbable characters and

145

outrageous incidents with the ring
of truth about them, the humor which
you are never absolutely sure is in-
tentional, the affectionate regard
which manages--most times--to stop
just short of sentimentality."[13]

Plowshare in Heaven - 1958
Helga Sandburg in the New York Herald-
Tribune Book Review: "Some of the stories
aren't stories; they are essays, on immortality mostly, on ghosts that favor Kentucky over Heaven. Mr. Stuart has command
of the language, and uses fine expressive
prose. He handles the flavored dialect
judiciously, so it comes across without
any sense of constraint upon the reader.
Putting down his book, it is as if one had
gone visiting in that stark and beautiful
land, had accepted a corner chair in one
of the single-room cabins, had shivered
when the wind moaned under the voice of
this teller of authentic tales."[14]

A Jesse Stuart Reader - 1963
(stories and poems)
Dorris Miller in the Huntington Herald
Advertiser: "Beauty and wonder, humor
and pathos innate in all human existence
are brought out in incidents in the lives
of dwellers in the Kentucky hills related
by a master of the story telling art."[15]

Between 1964 and 1968, Stuart published four
equally outstanding collections of short stories:
Save Every Lamb - 1964, A Jesse Stuart Harvest -
1965, My Land Has a Voice - 1966, Stories by Jesse
Stuart - 1968. In recent years, Stuart has published the following excellent collections of short
stories:

Come Gentle Spring - 1969
Dayton Rommel in the Chicago News:
"In a literary climate that encourages the
whine, the snarl and heavy breathing, Mr.
Stuart's muscular prose reaffirms the vigor
of American writing. It is exciting to

discover once again a writer with a point
of view, who neither deplores, anguishes,
excoriates, nor threatens."[16]

Come Back to the Farm - 1971
(stories and articles)
Ruel E. Foster in the Charleston Gazette-
Mail: "This latest book of Jesse Stuart
comes at a very opportune time. Today
all of us are much concerned with ecolog-
ical imbalances--with our vanishing air,
water, and land. But these admonitory
voices speaking up in the daily press
are really late comers. Jesse Stuart
long ago made his decision to stay with
the land--more specifically W-Hollow--
that pristine mountain spot, which has
become almost as famous as William
Faulkner's Yoknapatawpha County. . . .
Stuart is one of the very few writers in
this country today who can make use of
this mountain idiom with complete unself-
consciousness."[17]

Dawn of Remembered Spring - 1972
Barbara Zingman in the Louisville Times:
"Jesse Stuart performs magic. He gives
us a true sense of place--not only of our
region, but of our whole world. In his
latest collection of stories and poems
. . . Stuart evokes both the particular
quality of life found in the hills and
hollows of Eastern Kentucky and the universal feelings and emotions that all of
us share."[18]

32 Votes Before Breakfast - 1974
William Boozer in the Memphis Commercial
Appeal: "These stories are vintage
Stuart, at least seven of them as good
as Mark Twain at his best."[19]

But despite his unparalleled record, Stuart
has no more received his full due as a short story
writer than he has as a poet. There are two major
reasons this is so. One is the same cultural

prejudice that has hampered the reputation of his poetry. The other is the gradual erosion, underway for quite some time now, of the market for short stories and of the short story's role as a major literary form. Stuart has had a lot to say, perhaps more than any other author, on this devaluation of the short story.

Stuart has referred to the short story writer as the last independent craftsman left in the United States, but the craft is one he feels is rapidly disappearing in the face of a decreasing market and increasing demands that writers follow the latest fad. The story market of the 1930's was very different from that of the late 1960's, and the change has not been for the better.

In 1935 Stuart sold his first short stories to Story, American Mercury, Yale Review, and others and received over $1,000. In 1936 he sold one story for $1300, and in these years when readers were demanding good fiction Stuart received $10,000 in a single year for the sale of his short stories alone. The decline was sudden and has never been reversed. In 1946 Stuart sold short stories for fees ranging from $25 to $150 and, as was true of his experience in poetry, he believed he was through as a short story writer.[20]

These monetary values reflect what Stuart feels was a real shift in attitudes toward the short story in particular and toward original writing in general. With the fall of many prominent magazines, the mass market has become king, and young writers no longer have the outlets or the models that inspired Stuart as a young man:

Only a few magazines now use short stories. . . . Half of these have enough taboos to kill the originality of any writer. . . . All follow the policy of giving the reader what he wants, except a half dozen of the old literary magazines and quarterlies that have managed to survive the avalanche of mass circulation, highly organized, categorized reading habits of our people. I find myself belonging to the minority of

148

Americans who are still inclined to
prefer individualists to collectiv-
ists, skilled craftsmen to automatic
machines, and small farmers to fac-
tory farms.[21]

The lot of older writers dedicated to their
craft is no better. Stuart believes that the
field of creative writing has been invaded by
mass-thinking individuals and that many great
American authors have no market for their talents.
Those who will not conform to the latest fashion
must suffer financially: "Other original writers
like William Saroyan (who says he is so far in
debt he will never get out in his lifetime);
August Derleth (who is 57, has written over one
hundred books, and is in debt); James Still (one
of America's great stylists); Allan Tate (critic
and thinker); Donald Davidson (poet and critic);
Edgar Lee Masters (forty-five books and he died
penniless); and hundreds of other thinking American writers who are in debt, broke--live from
hand to mouth, and support themselves by teaching,
lecturing or doing something else. There is not
space for what they write."[22]

Despite this increasingly Orwellian literary
market, Jesse Stuart has announced his firm intention to continue writing highly individualistic
short stories in language any reader can understand;
he will not yield to "mass anything":[23] "I have
continued to write my kind of short stories, that
are different from most. I am the tree on which
these stories grow and I have held onto them like
the sere brown tough-butted white oak holds winter
leaves on its rugged boughs."[24]

The austere truth of Jesse Stuart's glum
picture of many publishers' increasing intolerance
of anything different in fiction was dramatically
indicated in _Esquire_ magazines' 40th _Anniversary
Celebration_ issue of October 1973; Jesse Stuart
was not among the thirty-nine authors included
despite the fact that Stuart had surpassed all
other writers in the number of his publications
in _Esquire_ magazine. Publisher Arnold Gingrich

149

observed of Stuart's conspicuous absence:

> Of course, everybody has his own favor-
> ites, and obviously they can't all be
> represented. My own would have been
> Jesse Stuart's "The Split Cherry Tree,"
> from our January, 1939, issue, a story
> that has been anthologized many more
> times than "The Snows of Kilimanjaro"
> (over a hundred and fifty times, in
> fact, and I noticed another request
> for permission to reprint it just last
> month), . . . Jesse Stuart's regional
> stories are, of course, out of synch
> with our current and recent New Fiction
> policies, but despite a paucity of ap-
> pearances in our pages over the last
> decade or so he ran up such a head
> start in the past, with fifty-eight
> printings since 1936, that his title
> as the magazine's champion contributor
> will not soon be threatened.[25]

Jesse Stuart's record of publication in
Esquire also included twenty-nine poems and two
articles for a combined total of eighty-nine
Stuart appearances since 1936.[26] The American
short-story artist from eastern Kentucky belonged
among the (for the most part) distinguished lite-
rati pictured on the foldout cover of Esquire's
40th edition. Just as much as Ernest Hemingway,
Thomas Wolfe, William Faulkner, F. Scott Fitzgerald,
and John Steinbeck, Jesse Stuart had paid his literary dues. Even if he has outlasted the short
story as a living commercial form, Stuart is as
much as any of these others the master of it.

Upon the basis of his incomparable record of
publication over the past forty years, Jesse Stuart
is undeniably one of America's greatest short story
authors. His hundreds of stories consistently appeared in the best literary and general magazines
in America and throughout the world. In addition,
his work has been repeatedly selected for inclusion
in hundreds of literary anthologies. Stuart knows
no superior in the history of the American short
story.

NOTES

1. Jesse Stuart, "How I Became a Novelist,"
   MS., Murray Kentucky University Library, p. 1.
   /Note: All manuscript references are to the
   massive Stuart collection at Murray Kentucky
   University/.

2. Jesse Stuart, untitled MS on how he became
   a writer, Murray Kentucky University Library,
   p. 31.

3. Jesse Stuart, "How My Short Stories are Born,"
   MS., Murray Kentucky University Library, p. 8.

4. Frank Hartwell Leavell, The Literary Career
   of Jesse Stuart (Ann Arbor Michigan: University Microfilms, Inc., 1965), p. 100.

5. Robert Van Gelder, "O'Brien Stories," New York
   Times, 16 June 1940, Sec. 6, pp. 6-7.

6. Harry Hansen, "The First Reader," review of
   Best American Short Stories, 1943, ed. by
   Martha Foley, in New York World-Telegram,
   Sept. 15, 1943.

7. William Peden, "The Best From 'Story': Is
   This the End?" review of Story Jubilee, ed.
   by Whit and Hallie Burnett, in Saint Louis
   Post Dispatch, May 9, 1965.

8. Jesse Stuart, untitled MS on the wide range
   of his short story publication, Murray Kentucky University Library, p. 25.

9. George Milburn, "The Kentucky Hills," review
   of Head o' W-Hollow, by Jesse Stuart, in
   New Republic, July 1, 1936, p. 248.

10. Ralph Thompson, "Books of the Times," review
    of Head o' W-Hollow, by Jesse Stuart, in
    New York Times, April 18, 1936, p. 13.

11. Milton Rugoff, "As Fresh as a Mountain Stream,"
    review of Men of the Mountains, by Jesse Stuart,

in New York Herald Tribune, March 16, 1941.

12. Nash K. Burger, "Twenty Tales, Regional and Readable," review of Dawn of Remembered Spring, by Jesse Stuart, in New York Times, Oct. 13, 1946, Sec. 7, p. 4.

13. Coleman Rosenberger, review of Clearing in the Sky and Other Stories, by Jesse Stuart, in New York Herald Tribune Book Review, Nov. 19, 1950, p.6.

14. Helga Sandburg, "Jesse Stuart's Tall Kentucky Tales," review of Plowshare in Heaven, by Jesse Stuart, in New York Herald Tribune Book Review, Sept. 14, 1958.

15. Dorris Miller, "Lasting Success Seen for Stuart Reader," review of A Jesse Stuart Reader, by Jesse Stuart, in Huntington (W. Va.) Herald Advertiser, August 25, 1963.

16. Dayton Rommel, "A breath of 'Spring', review of Come Gentle Spring, by Jesse Stuart, in Chicago News, June 28, 1969.

17. Ruel E. Foster, "Jesse Stuart still sings of the Land," review of Come Back to the Farm, by Jesse Stuart, in Charleston (W. Va.) Gazette-Mail, Nov. 14, 1971.

18. Barbara Zingman, "Stuart Collection is a Work of Magic," review of Dawn of Remembered Spring, by Jesse Stuart, in Louisville (Ky.) Times, April 5, 1972.

19. William Boozer, "In Touch with the Folks," review of 32 Votes Before Breakfast, by Jesse Stuart, in Memphis (Tenn.) Commercial Appeal, April 28, 1974, Sec. 6, p. 6.

20. Jesse Stuart, "The Last Independent Profession," Ball State University Forum, IX, No. 3 (Summer 1968), pp. 3-4.

21. Ibid., 6.

22. Ibid., 6-7.

23. Ibid., 7.

24. Ibid., 4.

25. Arnold Gingrich, Esquire, Oct. 1973, p. 10.

26. Boozer, "In Touch with the Folks," p. 6.

CHAPTER TEN

JESSE STUART--AMERICAN NOVELIST

"Writing the Great American Novel"

Jesse Stuart's novels are every bit as excellent as his poetry and short stories, just as beautifully crafted and just as profoundly universal in the scrupulous accuracy with which they present his particular experience of the world. Stuart has spoken of his novel writing almost as if it were automatic, using the same organic metaphors that he applies to his poems and short stories, but no one familiar with the full range of his work can doubt the back-breaking labor and clear guiding intelligence he brings to the job. "A story has to be born," he has said; characters take on a life of their own and are sometimes difficult to control.[1] He has described periods of incredible creativity (he once wrote 10,000 words of a novel in a single day).[2] "I write when I have to," he maintains, "like the time come for a birth."[3] But behind all these disavowals of conscious literary craftsmanship stands the record. Adding up his autobiographical and purely fictive books, Stuart has produced more novels of the first rank than anyone else of his generation. The gestation period of some of these books may have been subconscious, and they surely reflect an extraordinary genius, but no one could compile such a record without being a supremely disciplined and dedicated literary craftsman.

In assessing Stuart's achievement as a novelist, we face again the problem of sheer quantity. Some form of listing is the only way out of this difficulty. Here are Stuart's autobiographical novels along with selected reviews to show something of the impact each one had as it appeared:

Beyond Dark Hills - 1938
New York Times Book Review - "Beyond Dark Hills is, in its implication,

153

more than a personal record; it is
a chapter in the American story."[4]

The Thread That Runs So True - 1949
NEA Journal - "As 'the most important
book of 1949,' we name The Thread That
Runs So True by Jesse Stuart because
it is concerned with the unique insti-
tution which gives strength to all other
institutions in American life."[5]

The Year of My Rebirth - 1956
Time - "No man can really begin living
until he has come close to dying. That
is the message from Poet-Novelist Jesse
Stuart to his readers. . . . And implic-
it in the book is the strongly held feeling that the close brush with death was
well worth the cost."[6]

God's Oddling - 1960
Chicago Sunday Tribune Magazine of
Books - "Tributes often have been written
to mothers or fathers by their offspring
. . . but few have been so warm a picture
of a way of life, as well as of the subject of the portrait, as God's Oddling,
Jesse Stuart's book about his father.
. . . Of course, the story of Mick Stuart
also is the story of Jesse Stuart. To
admirers of that gifted writer, it is a
richer book for his own life being so
much a part of it."[7]

Mr. Gallion's School - 1967
Los Angeles Examiner - "In art as well
as in substance, Mr. Gallion's School
makes such educational novels as Up the
Down Stair Case and Blackboard Jungle
look like the frantic outpourings of
novices."[8]

To Teach, To Love - 1970
Worcester (Massachusetts) Telegram -
"Laden with charm and pleasantness, yet
provocative in its implications, enriched

by Stuart's sharing his private vision of true education, and set down
with a color and cadence that make it
a pleasure to read, this highly personal volume is absolutely enthralling."[9]

With the publication of Beyond Dark Hills,
some critics of rare insight realized that the
author was an American original and appreciated
his truly unique genius; such critics have periodically appeared throughout Stuart's career and
the depth of their insight has been no small
accomplishment, considering the fact that so
little has been and is known regarding the Appalachian subculture from which he writes. Beyond
Dark Hills has been established as one of the
greatest autobiographical novels of American
literature; it knows no superior. God's Oddling
is of equal caliber. It is infinitely more than
a son's great tribute to his father: it is an
archetypal tribute of all sons to all fathers.

The Thread That Runs So True has always been
considered a great biographical novel, but that
recognition barely scratches the surface of the
book's true significance. It is also part of a
trilogy, continued in Mr. Gallion's School and To
Teach, To Love, that still awaits critical discovery as the greatest treatment in American literature of our system of public education. These
three novels encompass American education from
first grade to graduate school and make up the
most eloquent argument ever presented for the
abiding importance of formal education in develop-
ing the character of Americans and America.

But even if Stuart's autobiographical works
were given the full measure of acclaim they de-
serve, the story of his achievement as a novelist
would be only half told. His purely fictional
books are equally imposing. Trees of Heaven, Taps
for Private Tussie, and Hie to the Hunters have
already been established as American classics by
major critics. But The Good Spirit of Laurel
Ridge, Mongrel Mettle, and Daughter of the Legend
have been inadequately dealt with and still await

155

significant critical interpretation. And there
are others. Once again, the only way to give a
good overview of Stuart's contributions to pure
fiction is to list them:

Trees of Heaven - 1940
News of Books and Authors - "He doesn't
like Gunther, take a continent for his
subject matter, nor rhapsodize for reams
about a railroad journey; but there is a
vastness and a spaciousness in this Ken-
tuckian's stuff which makes him, standing
in his fields in Kentucky, seem . . .
elemental . . . ."[10]

Taps for Private Tussie - 1943
Saturday Review - "The Southern poor white
has so often been portrayed in novels as
a hopelessly degenerate creature, invariably lazy, lecherous, and quarrelsome,
that he has become a stereotype in American fiction. . . . Jesse Stuart knows
his Southern mountaineers. He has grown
up among them; he can reproduce their talk
perfectly; and, despite their faults and
obvious shortcomings, he makes them out
to be engaging and warmly human people."[11]

Mongrel Mettle: The Autobiography of a
Dog - 1944
Chicago Tribune - "Jesse Stuart again
shows he's a master workman in this warm
hearted biography of a homely Kentucky
mongrel."[12] /No critic saw the possible
correlation between the word 'mongrel'
and the Appalachian subculture./

Foretaste of Glory - 1946
Saturday Review of Literature - "Every
one of these Blakesburg sketches has
something to tell us of the ways of
mankind, in a manner quite earthy and
realistic and unspoiled by an kind of
cliche. Stuart is an original observer,
as readers of his earlier books must
centainly already know."[13]

156

Hie to the Hunters - 1950
Atlantic Monthly - "It may well become
a classic of its kind."[14]

The Good Spirit of Laurel Ridge - 1953
/The vast majority of criticism is blatantly acculturated and of little rel-
evance._7

Daughter of the Legend - 1965
/Criticism is of little value. No critic
saw the possible interpretation of the
word "Melungeon" as a mask for the Appalachian subculture._7

The Land Beyond the River - 1973
/Land Beyond the River is a Jesse Stuart
satire of the welfare program of the
modern Welfare State._7

Hie to the Hunters has long been considered
a classic American novel, the equivalent of Tom
Sawyer or Huckleberry Finn. Taps for Private
Tussie was a Book of the Month Club Selection;
Trees of Heaven missed by only one vote.[15] Taps
was selected as a Masterpiece of World Literature
in 1952.[16] But Stuart still continued to be regarded by the majority of his critics as an untu-
tored and undisciplined local colorist. Even more
than his poetry, short stories, and autobiographical novels, Stuart's pure fiction has been
slighted by criticism. Particular books have been
appreciated by particular critics, but no sense of
Stuart's full stature as a writer of fiction has
yet emerged.

Daughter of the Legend, Mongrel Mettle, and
The Good Spirit of Laurel Ridge are all equally
fine books that have suffered by this lack of general esteem. If these novels had appeared under
the name of an acknowledged literary master, they
might have received the close attention they de-
serve and richly repay. They would have taken
their places beside Stuart's more famous works,
and the real scope of Stuart's achievement would
be more clearly seen. As it is, each of them still

awaits adequate criticism, and Stuart is widely
regarded as the writer of one or two good novels
and many weak ones. Assuming a knowledge of the
Appalachian subculture, perhaps an analysis of
Daughter of the Legend, one of Stuart's less admired works, will show how the critics have yet
to fully evaluate Stuart's accomplishments in
fiction.

Daughter of the Legend is a far more important Stuart novel than critics have credited it
with being. One critical consensus is that it is
a poor book because it is the only Stuart novel
set outside Kentucky and it is a "message" novel
dealing with the evils of racial segregation.[17]
A second critical approach views the book as cap-
turing rustic pleasures, vignettes of mountain
life, the essence of life lived close to nature,
and the ugly effects of ignorance, injustice and
hardship.[18] It is literally astonishing that no
critic of Daughter of the Legend has perceived
the possible interpretation of Stuart's racial
myth of the Melungeons as a mask for the Appalachian subculture and the prejudiced mistreatment
and stereotyping which Appalachians have traditionally received, and are receiving, at the hands
of the dominant culture.

Critics have emphasized the facts that Stuart
first became aware of the "Melungeon" racial myth
while he was a student at Lincoln Memorial University in Harrogate, Tennessee, and that the book's
Oak Hill is the actual Sneedville, Tennessee.
Early in the novel, Stuart's fictional Ben Dewberry
explains the four theories of Melungeon origin to
his friend Dave Stoneking, who has fallen deeply
in love with a Melungeon, Deutsia Huntoon: 1)
that the Melungeons are a mixture of Sir Walter
Raleigh's lost colony and the Cherokee Indians,
2) that the Melungeons are a mixture of early
Portugese sailors and Cherokees, 3) that the Melungeons are a mixture of poor mountain whites,
Indians and Negroes, 4) that the Melungeons are
a mixture of escaped slaves and trashy whites.[19]

One vital point critics of Daughter have overlooked is the fact that the book exposes the Melun-

geon myth as just that--a myth. In the environs of Oak Hill, "Melungeon" means a dark race of people--a people with dark skin, hair and eyes, but Deutsia Huntoon has blond hair and blue eyes! When Dave Stoneking marries Deutsia and lives among the Melungeons, he observes Melungeons with different-colored hair. Supposedly, Melungeons live on top of Sanctuary Mountain overlooking Oak Hill, but when Deutsia Huntoon's brothers conduct a Christmas hunt for the traditional turkey, they travel into the distant mountains of Virginia where they find hospitable fellow Melungeons who give them lodging for several nights. The reader has the feeling that they would have encountered similar Melungeons in the mountains of West Virginia, Kentucky, North Carolina, southern Pennsylvania, etc. Stuart thus destroys the racial myth before his reader's eyes and one rational question must inevitably follow: Who are these Melungeons? The answer is that they are the people of the traditional Appalachian subculture.

To appreciate Stuart's employment of Melungeon as a mask for Appalachian, it is necessary to remember the hill-valley dichotomy in the Appalachian subculture--the sharp social division between Appalachians who live on the hills and those who live in the valleys and towns. Appalachians of the valleys and towns possess more money and political clout, and they adopt the outlook of the dominant culture while Appalachians who live on the hills practice the traditional Appalachian way of life. Whenever inhabitants of the two worlds meet, the valley Appalachian becomes the embodiment of the dominant culture--passing judgments upon the traditional Appalachian subculture.

Dave Stoneking, narrator of Daughter of the Legend, is a "valley man" from Virginia, but he is that rare type of individual without cultural prejudice. As narrator of the novel, he stands on the borderline between the dominant American culture and the Appalachian subculture and gives the reader insight into the meaninglessness and tragedy that inevitably result from such superficial divisions of the family of man. Dave does cast his lot with Deutsia's hill people because of the valley people's treatment of him after he takes up residence on Sanctuary Mountain. As a result of his adoption of Deutsia's people, Dave loses his friend Ben Dewberry, his equal treatment under the law, his wife's life, and his cultural neutrality; he will fight for Deutsia's people for the rest of his life. At the end of the novel, Dave Stoneking has a new way of seeing--through the eyes of the hillmen of the Appalachian subculture.

Dave Stoneking and Ben Dewberry are valley Appalachians who grew up on adjoining farms in Wise County, Virginia. As young men they have been close friends working as lumberjacks in the mountains of North Carolina, Virginia and Tennessee. In Oak Hill, Tennessee, Ben falls in love with and marries Fern Hailston, a valley girl who is county health nurse. Her family owns a large dairy farm and is one of four families that run the county: the Hailstons, the Spools, the Holderbys and Old Judge Palmer (202). Dave Stoneking falls in love with Deutsia Huntoon, a Melungeon hillgirl whose people live in a shack on Sanctuary Mountain. Dave's persistence in loving Deutsia and his defense of her people's right to their way of life is the cause of the first disagreement between Dave and Ben, and their disagreement is a reflection of the conflict between the dominant American culture and the hillmen of the Appalachian subculture.

At Little Tavern in Oak Hill when Ben tells Fern that Dave is looking for a girl named Deutsia, the name causes the smile to leave Fern's face and her face to grow cold. Fern says that Deutsia never comes to Little Tavern and that she doesn't know Deutsia well. She blushes because the tavern crowd are listening to the conversation (6). Dave wonders why Fern doesn't like Deutsia--if there's been some kind of trouble between them or if they once loved the same man (7).

Deutsia later tells Dave that Little Tavern is not her side of town and Fern is not her kind of company (9). She tells him that Fern is, however, the only valley person who will climb the mountain to **deliver hill babies** and that Dave must forgive people for prejudices (19). When Dave decides to marry Deutisa, Ben Dewberry tells him that he shouldn't because she does not come from "good stock." Dave tells Ben that mountain people are every bit as good as valley people (29). When the townspeople of Oak Hill advise Dave not to marry a girl with Melungeon blood, Dave attacks and the cultural war is on: "I don't give a damn what kind of blood flows in Deutsia Huntoon's veins just so it isn't blue blood" (104).

Bass Huntoon, Deutsia's father, knows that this ancient war of acculturation is unto the death, and he makes certain that the valley man who marries his beloved Deutsia (his first born; his hunting and fishing companion; his fellow lover of the streams, flora and fauna, winds, moon and sun, ridges; and knower of many secrets not known in the valley below) is unmistakably aware of that fact. Bass says to Dave when Dave asks for Deutsia's hand in marriage—a formality not necessary in the traditional Appalachian subculture: "Do you know about us, and all the barriers against us? You'd better think this over before you jump from the frying pan into the fire. . . . I hope she doesn't get a husband that is prejudiced against her and her people. We've had enough to fight in our lifetime. And our children will have enough to fight. And maybe your children will have enough to fight" (117-118). This fight that Bass alludes to can, of course, be applied to the three generations of Appalachians in their twentieth-century fight to preserve their traditional culture.

In the beginning of the novel, Deutsia tells Dave that her mountain people are different from valley people:

> "You see the mountain?" Deutsia said
> to me as we'd walked fifty yards from
> the jail.
> "Yes."
> "We're a different people living
> there," she said.
> "Do you live there?"

161

"I do. That's Sanctuary Mountain."
"How are you a different people?"
"You'll have to learn." (14-15)

Throughout the remainder of their brief life
together, Dave learns that Deutsia's hill people
are different from valley people in treatment under
the law, education, closeness to the natural world,
interpretation of money, adaptation to modern technology, and tolerance of other cultural patterns
of behavior.

Early in the novel Dave leaves Fern and Ben
at Little Tavern and goes to search for Deutsia
at the Cantwell County Courthouse, a traditional
gathering place for Deutsia's people when they
come to town, because they have so many alter-
cations with "the Law." At the courthouse Dave
observes Deutsia's people--"tall, dark, swarthy,
sunburned, husky figures of the earth, fair women,
handsome men, bearded men with eagle eyes and old
women and mothers with deep-lined faces" (7).
Instead of the conventional food sold in Little
Tavern, Melungeon women outside the courthouse
sell turtle-steak, fish, home-cured-ham, and rab-
bit sandwiches, with wine and lemonade as bever-
ages (8). If these are not Stuart's Appalachian
hill people, then they never have existed.

As Dave accompanies Deutsia to visit Don
Praytor, a hill man in jail, Dave shakes the jailer's hand, a "soft shrivelled cold hand that felt
like a cold-blooded blacksnake" (10). When Dave
asks Deutsia why Don Praytor, a Melungeon and father of five children is in jail, Deutsia explains
the unequal treatment her people have received
under the law: "If you live in the valley and
make whiskey," she said, "You don't go to jail.
If you live up on the mountain where I live and
if you are even found with whiskey on you, you go
to jail" (12). The county sheriff discovered a
half-pint of whiskey on Don and he has been in
jail eight months without a trial; the jailor receives a dollar a day for each prisoner (12).

Deutsia brings Don sandwiches and wine, tel-

162

ling him "all this came from the mountain" (13).
She knows the food and drink will restore his
soul.   Later in the novel Dave meets Don Praytor
at Don's home on Sanctuary Mountain and asks him
if he ever stood trial.   Don tells Dave that he
did not--that he faked insanity by hiding little
pieces of tobacco all over his jail cell and
shouting, "No son-of-a-bitch will ever find that"
and the jailor released him immediately (68).
Don suspects that Dave, by caring enough to ask
about his injustice, is not a valley person: "You
aint from the valley, are you?"   Dave replies:
"No, I'm from the mountains," . . . "The Virginia
mountains" (68).

Through a bigotted process of guilt by association, Dave experiences the same raw edge of the
law as his adopted hill people.   When Mr. Woods,
the county clerk, refuses to grant Dave and Deutsia
a marriage license, Dave shouts, "I thought this
was a free country," and Woods shows Dave a .38
Special (124).   Dave tells circuit judge John
Palmer that there are laws against treating the
mountain men the way the judge and his cronies do,
and the furious judge voices the worst valley
stereotypes of hill people: "They're an ignorant
people.   They have no morals either and . . ."
Dave interrupts the judge and informs him that
hill people have a different kind of education
than valley people:

> "Judge Palmer, they are educated in
> their way," I interrupted him.   I couldn't
> stand for him to talk this way about them.
> He was the one who was ignorant.   "They
> don't have book education because they've
> been denied schooling in the Valley and
> the missionary teachers, outsiders called
> Presbyterians who believe Melungeons are
> God's children too, walk up that mountain
> and teach them up to the eighth grade in
> pitiful log-shack schoolhouses while
> Valley children can go to high school and
> then on to college.   No, they're not edu-
> cated in books like you, but they know
> Sanctuary Mountain and everything that

lives and grows on it and they know the
streams and the rivers and signs in the
skies. They know when and how and where
to plant their patches and to harvest
them, where bee trees are and how to find
them and where wild game is and how to
catch it for food. They know the holes
in Clinch River where the big fish live.
I'm married to a Melungeon and I know
how smart they are." (159-160)

Deutsia explains to Dave the traditional in-
equity of hill children in the process of formal
education. She says that the only reason that
Cantwell County school teachers come to the mountain, with one exception, is because they cannot
find a school elsewhere. Deutsia says that one
teacher was beloved by the hill people because
she came out of a motive of love. When Dave asks
if the teacher were like the valley people, Deutsia
replies: "No, she loved us, helped us, taught us,
and we loved her" (187). Deutsia tells Dave that
this beloved teacher died on the mountain, her
tombstone was erected by mountain people, and each
spring on Decoration Day school children decorate
her grave with baskets of wild flowers (188).

Dave comes to see that Deutsia's mountain
people, of less formal education than valley people, have a closer attachment to nature and the
land. Deutsia knows the flora, fauna, geography,
and all the secrets of her mountain (54). In typical Appalachian tradition, her people doctor themselves with herbs and believe the phases of the
moon have power over their lives and crops. Their
food is from their earth--wild game, canned wild
fruits, garden vegetables, milk, honey and wine
(114-115). Dave and Deutsia's life is patterned
after the traditional Appalachian hillside farm
way of life (131). Deutsia's religion is the wild
beauty of nature: the moon and stars or a spring
walk in April's renewal of the mountain, breaking
the death of winter (221).

After associating with Deutsia's tall figures
of earth, Dave Stoneking comes to understand their
great love of and closeness to the land of their

birth. With the cool December wind of the mountain upon his face, Dave, after leaving the cultural hypocrisy he has just experienced in Oak Hill, knows why Sanctuary Mountain is so dear to Melungeons; he feels that he belongs there rather than with the valley people (166-167).

During his brief acculturation as a Melungeon, Dave sees that the hill people, unlike valley people, place absolutely no emphasis upon money. In sharp contrast, Dave notices that once his friend Ben Dewberry decided to marry Fern and be a big valley farmer time became the equivalent of money to him (64-65). Dave further notices that money plays a role in Ben's and Fern's love that it does not play in his and Deutsia's: "Money meant a lot to Fern Hailston and Ben Dewberry: money was their substitute for love" (103). Dave observes the happiness of the whole Huntoon family on Christmas day, following their exchange of humble gifts from the mountain, and notices that the Huntoons do not correlate money and happiness: "The Huntoons were a happy family. They had love for each other and they were as free as mountain winds. I thought of my home in Virginia. My father and mother didn't believe in smoking and they certainly didn't believe in drinking. We lived better than the Huntoons, but we never had as much fun as they had. Now the kitchen was filled with smoke, for everybody was smoking but little Cress, and if he had asked for a cigarette, I believe Bass and Daid would have given it to him" (184).

Deutsia's and Dave's hill people do not impose their value system upon valley people, but they must fight continuously against the cultural pressure exerted by valley people against them. Different spokesmen throughout Daughter clearly state that highland Appalachians will remain Appalachians despite all the forces of acculturation that the dominant culture can bring against them. These are some of the most moving statements of cultural protest in American literature.

Dave tells Deutsia that in this long feud between valley people and hill people he will

fight for her mountain people until the bitter
end and their troubles will become his troubles
(15). Hunt Mallicoat, the square dance caller at
the Huntoon's house on the night of Dave and
Deutsia's wedding, speaks to the fiddle, guitar,
and banjo players and the waiting dancers: "Every
one of ye. Hear me! I mean it. Let this be a
night of enjoyment! Let us feast and be happy
tonight! Like a tough-butted white oak that grows
on this mountain, we will not be whipped! But by
the music we will be moved! Don't ye doubt it"
(137).

From these and many additional parallels, one
discovers that Jesse Stuart's "Melungeons" are a
mask for the three generations of the Appalachian
hill people of the twentieth century. Nearly all
the older Melungeon men have beards and women wear
long hair that falls down their backs (108); portraits of old people in Melungeon homes look like
people from a different world (110); and Melungeons
are very adept at making homemade crazy-patched
quilts and rugs (109-110).

At the end of Daughter of the Legend, Deutsia
Huntoon resolves the myth of Melungeon blood color
by hemorrhaging to death in rich red pools of blood
while giving birth to David Huntoon Stoneking--who
is symbolic of the union of the dominant American
culture and the Appalachian subculture that can be
accomplished through love and understanding. Ben
and Fern do come and try to help save Deutsia's
life and Ben tells Dave that he and Fern are going
to start acting like they feel, even if they have
to move from the valley and build a new home on
the mountain. Ben tells Dave that there is too
much trouble in the world for them to be divided
(240).

Following Deutsia's death Dave is in the unique position of deciding which of two cultures his
son will be reared in. Deutsia had not been highly
educated but she had been the most loving person
Dave had ever known; Deutsia lacked money but she
was completely happy and one with the great natural
rhythms of the land of her birth; and Deutsia simply

lived her life without imposing her ways upon other people. Dave could take his son to be reared in his parents' home in Virginia, but he leaves him to be reared by Bass and Daid Huntoon: "The decision didn't come easy. I'd had dreams of our son going with his mother and me to the woods at night and walking the paths and leaping the streams in the moonlight. I wanted him to grow up as his mother had grown up in the freedom of Sanctuary Mountain. I wanted him to know the changing seasons, to know the powers of the sun, the magic of the moon and the taste, smell and feel of the wind. I wanted him to interpret the sounds of the wind as Deutsia and her people had done for a century. I wanted him to know and love the night as his Melungeon ancestors did" (247).

Daughter of the Legend is not a minor novel, nor is it the work of a local colorist. It is like the bulk of Stuart's writing in its absolute truth to the particular, but also in the deeper significance it achieves. With its narrator strategically located on the borderline between cultures, the novel is able to explore the subject of intolerance from both sides at the same time. Once the metaphor of the "Melungeons" is penetrated, the book can be seen as a deeply felt commentary on the plight of traditional Appalachia, one of the nation's largest subcultures. But it is the poetry of its style and the powerful realization of its protagonists' experience that make Daughter of the Legend a fine work of fiction. By involving us profoundly with his characters and their world, Stuart makes us feel the force of his thesis directly--we discover in our own reactions how cultural differences can pale before our common humanity.

When one realizes that in his autobiographical and fictional novels Jesse Stuart has embodied all the cultural indices long before they had been thought of; that Stuart's fictional embodiment of the Appalachian subculture is without rival and reflects the irreversible impact the dominant culture has had; and that Stuart's narrators narrate from a borderline between the two cultures--one comprehends Stuart's genius and complexity as one of America's greatest novelists.

167

NOTES

1. Jesse Stuart, "How to Write the Great American Novel and The Probable Results," MS, Murray Kentucky University Library, pp. 1-2. /Note: All manuscript references are to the massive Stuart collection at Murray Kentucky University/.

2. Jesse Stuart, "How I Became a Novelist," MS, Murray Kentucky University Library, p. 2.

3. Betty Garrett, "An Appalachian Author Describes His Life Style," Appalachia 6 (Dec. 1972-Jan. 1973), 28.

4. J. Donald Adams, "Jesse Stuart's Homespun Story," review of Beyond Dark Hills, by Jesse Stuart, in New York Times Book Review, April 24, 1938, pp. 24-25.

5. Joy Elmer Morgan, "The Thread That Runs So True," NEA Journal, XXVIII (Jan. 1950), 7.

6. "Coronary," review of The Year of My Rebirth, by Jesse Stuart, in Time, Dec. 24, 1956, p. 62.

7. Fanny Butcher, "Son's Poetic and Amusing Tribute to Father," review of God's Oddling by Jesse Stuart, in Chicago Sunday Tribune Magazine of Books, Nov. 20, 1960, p. 3.

8. H. Edward Richardson, "Reviews of Mr. Gallion's School," review of Mr. Gallion's School, by Jesse Stuart, in Los Angeles Examiner, July 28, 1968, p. 13.

9. Sigmund A. Lavine, "Rewards of Teaching," review of To Teach, To Love, by Jesse Stuart, in Worcester (Mass.) Telegram, Feb. 1, 1970.

10. Whit Burnett, "'An Event,' Is Jesse Stuart's First Novel," review of Trees of Heaven, by Jesse Stuart, in News of Books and Authors, Mar.-Apr. 1940.

11. Philip Van Doren Stern, "Stuart's Incorrigible Tussies," review of Taps for Private Tussie, by Jesse Stuart, in Saturday Review, Nov. 27, 1943, p. 6.

12. Bob Becker, "Jerry Was One Mutt Who Really Was a Gay Dog," review of Mongrel Mettle, by Jesse Stuart, in Chicago Tribune, Feb. 20, 1944.

13. Nathan L. Rothman, "On the Eve of the World's End," review of Foretaste of Glory, by Jesse Stuart, in Saturday Review of Literature, March 9, 1946, p. 12.

14. "Hie to the Hunters," review of Hie to the Hunters, by Jesse Stuart, in Atlantic Monthly, March 1950.

15. Frank Hartwell Leavell, The Literary Career of Jesse Stuart (Ann Arbor, Michigan: University Microfilms, 1965), pp. 109-111.

16. Ish Richey, Kentucky Literature (Tompkinsville, Kentucky: Monroe County Press, 1963), p. 165.

17. Ruel E. Foster, Jesse Stuart (New York: Twayne Publishers, Inc., 1968), p. 146.

18. Mary Washington Clarke, "The Voice of Jesse Stuart," review of Daughter of the Legend, by Jesse Stuart, in American Book Collector, Feb. 1966, p. 4.

19. Jesse Stuart, Daughter of The Legend (New York: McGraw Hill, 1965), p. 78.

Jesse and Naomi at home in W-Hollow--1970

CHAPTER ELEVEN

STUART'S POSITION
IN AMERICAN LITERATURE

Jesse Stuart's position as a major figure has
yet to be recorded in the majority of critical
books dealing with American authors. The South
Since Appomattox and Writers in the Modern World
are, regrettably, only too typical of the great
injustice done to Jesse Stuart. In The South Since
Appomattox, Thomas D. Clark and Albert D. Kirwain
write of Thomas Wolfe, a native of Asheville, North
Carolina, as a giant in both physical and literary
dimensions. They then refer to the readily dis-
cernible provincialism of Faulkner's novels but
grant his writing broad universality in that the
author's characters and scenes from central and
northern Mississippi show a great awareness of
folk culture, a deeply ingrained sense of humor,
and an instinctive feeling for violence and human
frustration and what results they produce. Jesse
Stuart is appraised in the following manner:

> On the bank of the Ohio where the shoulder
> of the Cumberland Plateau nudges the great
> river off its direct course, Jesse Stuart
> has revealed the deep emotional attach-
> ment of man for the soil, and revealed the
> basic struggle of the individual to subdue
> the forces of nature long enough to extract
> some of the meager satisfactions from life
> itself. With less harshness, but no less
> humorous vigor, Stuart's Man With a Bull-
> Tongue Plow (1934) Beyond Dark Hills (1938)
> and Taps for Private Tussie (1944) reflect
> a rural pattern closely akin in sentimen-
> tality, if not in fact, to that of the
> agrarianism of the Fugitives of Nashville.[1]

Donald Davidson, in Southern Writers in the
Modern World, refers to Stuart's hitchhiking to
Vanderbilt with very little money and trying to
live on eleven meals a week, but dodges assessment

171

except to vaguely maintain that Vanderbilt must have had "some" influence on Stuart's literary art.[2] But perhaps Allen Tate's statement to Davidson as to why he /Tate7 would not include Stuart material in The House of Fiction (1950) most clearly reveals the kind of blatant critical injustice Stuart has suffered because of cultural prejudice: "I suppose prejudice explains our omission of Jesse Stuart. His dramatization of himself as the Hill-billy, for New York consumption, has disgusted me for years, and I suppose I can't be fair to his work."[3]

Fortunately, throughout Jesse Stuart's career there have always been some critics appreciative of his truly unique genius. Most recently Stuart has been selected for inclusion in American Fiction 1900-1950 as among 44 of the important writers of the first half of the twentieth century--based upon the critical esteem given to them and to their work. This book, edited by Professor James Woodress, chairman of the English department at University of California at Davis, is to be the first in a series of more than 50 volumes--intended as a source guide in American literature, English literature, and world literature in English.[4] In late 1975 Jesse Stuart was informed by McGraw Hill that The World of Jesse Stuart, the most recent collection of Stuart poems, had been nominated for a Pulitzer Prize.[5]

But Stuart's claim to greatness is not really based on the opinions of his critics. His position as a major American author has long been established by his millions of readers throughout America and the world. Stuart's work appears in more than two hundred and twenty-five anthologies of American literature.[6] His work has been translated and can be found in libraries in the countries of Europe; in the Arabic countries; in the French speaking countries of Africa; in Egypt, Israel, Lebanon, Iran, West Pakistan, Bangladesh, The Phillipines, Taiwan, Korea, and Japan; in the Spanish speaking countries of South America; in Russia; and in Australia--on six of the earth's continents.

In 1975 Jesse Stuart looked back at his long writing career, one of the most prodigious and successful in the history of American literature:

> My mission had been completed. I knew what I was going to try to do. I would send my Appalachia over America and to the world. Since I left Vanderbilt, spring '32, until this present hour, February 14th, 1975, I have had 44 books published, 470 stories, 2100 poems, 400 articles, over 3,000 publications listed by Dr. Hensley Woodbridge in his Bibliography of my creativity. I've traveled in 49 states of America (Alaska excluded) and lectured extensively in 45 states. In a dozen states I've spoken no less than 100 times.
> I've traveled in 90 countries, my wife in 70 with me. I've lectured over and worked in nine foreign countries.[7]

At the very beginning of Stuart's literary career, William Saroyan (as has been true of other of Stuart's fellow American literary artists throughout his career) recognized Jesse Stuart as a truly unique literary genius:

> As I see it, Jesse Stuart is a natural. A natural is somebody who could be nobody very gracefully but happens to have genius, and is therefore somebody, very gracefully. He is anonymous and a personage at the same time. Any person capable of genius and anonymity simultaneously is a person who is truly great. In his greatness is no element of stress, and in Stuart's greatness there is no stress. It is a casual, easy-going greatness. Such a greatness in a writer means better, simpler and more durable writing. It means naturalness. Stuart is one of the most natural writers in the country. I think of him as an American Robert Burns. He is not a city-made writer, and in him is none

of the irritation and confusion of the
city-made writer. He is, and the people of his writing are, real against a
natural, not an artificial background.[8]

Anyone could have traveled in Jesse Stuart's
W-Hollow from the 1930's until the present time.
Such a traveler could ramble from Shackle Mill
Run, to the Big Sandy, to the Little Sandy, and to
Greenup. He would see many picturesque old men
but never Op Akers. He would see many hard working farmers but never Sal and Little Mitch Powderjay. He would see many young lovers but never
Tarvin Bushman and Subrinea Tussie. He perhaps
might hear a fine mountain fiddler but never the
likes of Uncle George Tussie:

> "I've played summers for you," Uncle
> George said. "I've played autumn for
> you with the wind a-rustlin down the dead
> leaves from the trees and a-blowin through
> the dead grasses; I've played the last
> notes of the grasshoppers, the katydids
> and the bettles. Now I'm a-goin to play
> winter for you. You'll be able to hear
> the winter wind around this shack--the
> winter wind a-blowin high among the leaf-
> less oak tops and a-moanin among the thick
> needles on the tall pine trees. Winter is
> a sad time and I love to play winter tunes.
> Listen for the snowbirds a-chirrupin among
> the dead ragweeds and pickin up ragweed
> seeds from the snow. Listen to 'em
> a-nestin in the fodder shocks."
> . . . .
> I wondered how on earth this big rough-
> lookin man like Uncle George could drag
> from his fiddle strings such pretty music
> by just fingerin the strings with his long
> fingers and a-drawin the bow across the
> strings. How could he get such pretty
> music from the winter world? You could
> hear the fallin of the snowflakes as they
> preened against the oak leaves still a-
> clingin to the tough-butted white oaks.
> You could hear the hungry snowbirds a-

chirrupin as they found ragweed seeds
upon the snow and picked them up to
fill their craws. You could hear the
birds' tiny bills a-peckin against the
hard crust of snow and after a while
you could hear their satisfied chirrupin. Then you heard 'em a-flyin to
the fodder shocks, through the icy
winter wind. And as they roosted in
the fodder shocks, you could hear them
rustle the fodder blades. Uncle George
could make the sounds on his fiddle for
he went to the cornfield in winter and
heard the wind among the fodder shocks
and mocked it with his fiddle. And it
was lonesome to hear the high wind in
the leafless oak tops and to hear it
blow among the thick pine needles.[9]

A traveler in Appalachia would not see such characters because they never have and never will
exist except in the mind and works of a literary
genius. No traveler will ever hear a fiddler like
Uncle George because George fiddles nothing--a
great master of American literature draws the bow
across the strings.

On the night of Jesse Stuart's birth in an
humble log cabin in the Appalachian world of W-
Hollow--the stars in the heavens must surely have
been in unique alignment. The rocky fields of
New England brought forth and spoke through Robert
Frost. The deep South delta country brought forth
and spoke through William Faulkner. Appalachia
brought forth and has spoken through Jesse Stuart.

Granted this Appalachian background, Jesse
Stuart of Kentucky is a major American author in
poetry, the short story, and the autobiographical
and fictional novel. The world of W-Hollow is his
Appalachian Dublin and Jefferson, and Stuart writes
from his hill-rimmed locale to the world. Stuart
is a literary genius and major American author not
in spite of his artistic use of the Appalachian
culture but because of it.

Jesse Stuart must no longer wait for critics

to rule him inside or outside American literature
as a major American author. He is already inside
where he is a permanent fixture. As is true of
all major American authors, Jesse Stuart occupies
a position in American literature that is unique
and secure forever:

No one has sung for us and may I sing
As one of us, for all of us my songs
Though futile as the mountain winds that fling
Their fluffy bellies on these throngs
Of jutted hills oak-crowned against the skies.
I sing of mountain men, their lives and loves
And mountain waters and the wild-bird cries,
The percoon blooming in the late March coves.
It's fun to run on iron legs and shout
Songs to the wind my blood has left unsung,
The times at home they never thought about
Too busy living life while they are young.
I'll keep on singing long as this blood flows
And brain keeps active in this living head;
I'd like eternal spring when this blood goes
To sing among ghosts of the mountain dead.[10]

NOTES

1. Thomas D. Clark and Albert D. Kirwain, _The South Since Appomattox / A Century of Regional Change_ (New York: Oxford University Press, 1967), pp. 222-224.

2. Donald Davidson, _Southern Writers in the Modern World_, (Athens: University of Georgia Press, 1958), pp. 65-66.

3. John Tyrell Fain and Thomas Daniel Young, eds., _The Literary Correspondence of Donald Davidson and Allen Tate_ (Athens: The University of Georgia Press, 1974), p. 351.

4. Thelma Scott Kiser, "Jesse Stuart in 'American Fiction, 1900-1950'," review of _American Fiction, 1900-1950_, ed. by James Woodress, in Ashland (Ky.) _Daily Independent_, Feb. 9, 1975, p. 14.

5. "Kentucky Poet," Bowling Green (Ky.) _Park City Daily News_, 28 Oct. 1975, p. 4.

6. Anthologies, pp. 1-9. A listing of anthologies containing works by Jesse Stuart in the Stuart collection at Murray Kentucky University Library.

7. Jesse Stuart, untitled MS, pp. 2, 30-31, in the Stuart collection at Murray Kentucky University Library.

8. William Saroyan, "Time Out For Jesse Stuart," _News of Books and Authors_ II (Mar.-Apr. 1940).

9. Jesse Stuart, _Taps for Private Tussie_ (New York: The World Publishing Company, 1969), pp. 247-248.

10. Jesse Stuart, _Beyond Dark Hills_ (New York: E. P. Dutton, 1938), p. 379.

Jesse Stuart's birthplace in W-Hollow, Kentucky

SELECTED BIBLIOGRAPHY

Blair, Everetta Love, Jesse Stuart; His Life and
Works. Columbia, South Carolina: University
of South Carolina Press, 1967.

Caudill, Harry M., Night Comes to the Cumberlands.
Boston, Massachusetts: Little, Brown & Co., 1962.

Clarke, Mary Washington, Jesse Stuart's Kentucky.
New York: McGraw-Hill, 1968.

Foster, Ruel E., Jesse Stuart. New York: Twayne
Publishers, Inc., 1968.

Hall, Edward T., The Silent Language. New York:
Fawcett World Library, 1963.

Hall, Wade, "The Truth is Funny": A Study of
Jesse Stuart's Humor. Terre Haute, Indiana,
Indiana Council of Teachers of English, Indiana
State University, 1970, 75 pp., Vol. 5, pt. 1,
nos. 2-4 of the Indiana English Journal.

Leavell, Frank, The Literary Career of Jesse Stuart.
Ann Arbor, Michigan: University Microfilms, Inc.,
1965.

LeMaster, J. R. ed., Jesse Stuart: Selected Criticism. St. Petersburg, Florida: Valkyrie Press,
Inc., 1978.

LeMaster, J. R. & Mary Washington Clarke, eds.,
Jesse Stuart: Essays on His Work. Lexington,
Kentucky: The University Press of Kentucky, 1977.

Pearsall, Marion, Little Smoky Ridge: The Natural
History of a Southern Appalachian Neighborhood.
University, Alabama: University of Alabama Press,
1959.

Pennington, Lee, The Dark Hills of Jesse Stuart; A
Consideration of Symbolism and Vision in the
Novels of Jesse Stuart. Cincinnati, Ohio:
Harvest Press, The Kentucky Writers' Guild, 1967.

179

Perry, Dick, _Reflections of Jesse Stuart On A Land of Many Moons_. New York: McGraw-Hill Book Co., 1971.

Maurer, David W., _Whiz Mob_. University of Florida, Gainesville, Florida: American Dialect Society, 1955.

Trager, George L., "Language in Culture." _Encyclopedia Britannica_, 1955 ed.

Walls, David S. & John B. Stephenson, eds., _Appalachia in the Sixties_. Lexington, Kentucky: The University Press of Kentucky, 1972.

Weller, Jack E., _Yesterday's People_. Lexington, Kentucky: The University of Kentucky Press, 1965.

Woodbridge, Hensley C., _Jesse and Jane Stuart: A Bibliography_. Murray, Kentucky: Murray State University Printing Services, 1979.